IN Style

Top Image Experts Reveal Strategies
to Always Look and Be Your Best

PowerDynamics
PUBLISHING

PowerDynamics Publishing
San Francisco, California
www.powerdynamicspub.com

ISBN: 978-0-9644906-7-3

Library of Congress Control Number: 2010904074

Printed in the United States of America on acid-free paper.

We dedicate this book to you, the woman who understands the value of presenting a stylish appearance.
We know that you want to enhance your own style and that you are ready to step into an inspired new vision of yourself—and we celebrate you!

The Co-Authors of Inspired Style

TABLE *of* CONTENTS

ACKNOWLEDGEMENTS

Gratitude looks good on everyone. Before we share our wisdom and experience with you, we have a few people to thank for turning our vision for this book into a reality.

This book was the brilliant concept of Caterina Rando, an image enthusiast and the founder of PowerDynamics Publishing. As a respected business strategist who works with image professionals to grow their businesses, she realized how much she was learning about color, shapes, accessorizing and putting together a great wardrobe and wanted more women to benefit from our wisdom. The result was putting our tips and strategies into this comprehensive book.

Without Caterina's "take action" spirit, her commitment to excellence and her highly skilled professional publishing team, you would not be reading this book, of which we are all so proud. Our truly dedicated team worked diligently to put together the best possible book for you. We are truly grateful for everyone's stellar contribution.

To Bernie Burson, whose experience in copywriting and copyediting proved invaluable, and whose magic pen and image expertise ensured that this book would be the best it could be.

To LynAnn King, whose positive energy, creativity and image industry savvy provided valuable support, we are truly grateful.

To Ruth Schwartz, with her many years of experience and wisdom, who served as an ongoing guide throughout the project. Your support to our production team and to all of the co-authors is deeply appreciated.

To Julie Maeder, who in addition to being a co-author also brought her creative talent to the cover design. We say thank you for a job well done.

Our book layout looks simple and elegant as a result of the efforts of Barbara McDonald, who brought enthusiasm, problem-solving and her attention to detail to this project.

To Karen Gargiulo who provided us with a keen eye to punctuation and grammar and an elegant touch to clarity, thank you for your support and contribution.

We also acknowledge each other for delivering outstanding information, guidance and advice. Through our work in this book and with our clients, we are truly committed to enhancing the lives of women through the skills of style. We are truly grateful that we get to do work that we love and make a contribution to so many in the process. We do not take our good fortune lightly. We are clear in our mission—to make a genuine contribution to you, the reader. Thank you for granting us this extraordinary opportunity.

The Co-Authors of Inspired Style

INTRODUCTION

Congratulations! You have opened an incredible resource, packed with great ideas that will boost your style quotient in ways you cannot yet imagine. You are about to discover the magic of *Inspired Style.*

Your personal style is so much more than clothes and fashion. As image consultants, our first concern is to understand you and what makes you the unique person you are. Only then can we begin to help you achieve the distinctive look and style that conveys your authentic self. Several chapters will lead you on this journey of self-discovery.

Then, you can use this book to quickly rev up your style, because as top experts in each of our respective specialties, we've joined together to give you the most helpful image strategies we know. Some bits of advice are repeated in different chapters—but that should tell you how important that advice is!

Each of us has seen how even small changes in your personal image can improve your self-confidence and uplift your spirit. A gorgeous new accessory in your signature color can transform several outfits and make you feel like a million. Learning the secrets of emphasizing your positives, dressing for your body type and learning to move like a confident queen can make a world of difference in the way the world perceives you.

To get the most out of this book, we recommend that you read through it once, cover to cover. Then go back and follow the tips that apply to you, in the chapters most relevant to your current situation. Every image improvement you make will make a difference in how you feel and in how others respond to you.

Know that just learning the how-tos will not transform your style. You must take action, consider your style motivation and apply the strategies, tips and tactics we share in these pages. Do the exercises and apply the many ideas in this book and you will reap many rewards. With our knowledge and your action, we are confident that, like our thousands of satisfied clients, you too will master the magic of *Inspired Style.*

To your fabulous new style!

The Co-Authors of Inspired Style

The Law *of* Attrac*tive*
Because Looking the Part is Half the Battle

By Cheryl Obermiller

$\mathcal{M}$y grandmothers were always great sources of wisdom, much of which they expressed through old sayings. Some were helpful, like "Never sleep on your anger." Some were out-dated like, "My father said nice girls don't wear short hair." Others just weren't quite true. My face did not freeze like that, and children born on Monday were no more filled with woe than anyone else. (If you didn't understand that, go ask your grandmother.) However, one that I still find confusing is, "Never judge a book by its cover." What, then, are we supposed to judge them on and why do publishers pay so much attention to the covers? In reality, the cover matters a great deal and we will likely be unhappy if that cover has misled us about the contents.

Most of us understand that what we see on the outside of something is a pretty strong indicator of what we will find on the inside. So, what do people see on our covers? What do they think they will find inside us? And more important, is the image we see in the mirror one that shows who we really are and that will help us achieve our goals and strengthen our relationships? It can be!

We all have to face this simple fact: looks matter, and they matter a lot. Furthermore, really powerful appearances don't happen by accident. Unless we take a moment to think about how we want to look, we are likely to just grab old favorites out of habit, even if they are not appropriate to our goals or activities of the day. Sometimes I get so busy with life that instead of making intelligent decisions about what I should wear, I fall into the same habit as the late comedienne, Gilda Radner, who said, "I base most of my fashion sense on what doesn't itch." What exciting things might await us if instead we got dressed with a little more planning and a little less randomness? Maybe if we think about what we need to achieve that day we could ask more important questions than "Does this make me look fat?" Perhaps the big question could be, "Does this make me look like the person I want to be and send the message I want to send?"

One of the most common reactions I get when people find out that I am an image consultant is that they ask things like, "Do I look okay? I think this is an attractive outfit, but what do you think?" Now, I don't mind giving out a little free advice, but I do think that we could all help ourselves by becoming more fluent in the language of image. We can know for ourselves that we not only look good, but that we look like the competent, capable women we really are. Deliberate, intelligent management of our personal style is about honesty, individuality, freedom and excitement! It is knowing that we can express our moods, interests and goals in a beautiful variety of ways. But that is not all.

When we think of being "attractive," we usually think of looking pretty. That is fine, but image has a dynamic influence on our relationships, opportunities and incomes. Whatever your image currently is, for better or worse, it is attractive. The real question is, "Attractive to what?" Is it attractive to respect, wealth and love, or to something less desirable?

Most people today, whether they embrace it or not, have heard about The Law of Attraction—the belief that we can use focused mental energy to help get what we want. However, many neglect one of the most powerful and quickly achieved vehicles to personal success available, without even knowing it. What is it?

The Law of Attrac*tive*

A dynamically attractive personal image—which includes intelligent choices in dress, grooming, body language and etiquette—can act as a magnet to help attract success. It can also be the catalyst that turbo charges progress by clearly showing that you mean business! How? By dynamically sending your chosen message to everyone who sees you. Additional job training, internships and so on, may be necessary components of success, but they are also time-consuming. However, you can see the effects of a dynamically attractive image almost immediately. In fact, by this time tomorrow you can look and feel closer to your goals than you do today! This is true even if what you consider natural beauty is not your greatest asset.

Three Keys to Putting The Law of Attrac*tive* to Work For You

1. Establish Credibility

"Seldom do people discern eloquence under a threadbare cloak."
—Juvenal, 1st Century Roman poet

This is an old-fashioned way of saying, "It is hard for me to believe you are as good as you say you are, when you look like kind of a mess." When what you say, and how you appear are not in harmony, people will almost always believe that what they see is the truth.

What does the word *threadbare* mean today, to you? Some modern words are *worn out, dirty, in poor repair, sloppy* and *dated.*

One critical thing to consider when evaluating your image is that nothing will destroy credibility faster than poor hygiene and grooming. For example, you either wear nail polish, or dye your hair, or you don't. If you don't have time to keep these things up, then just go for clean and neat.

Cleanliness and neatness will also make even a humble wardrobe highly attractive. Keep buttons sewn on, repair loose hemlines and clean clothing regularly. Even a wardrobe that comes from a thrift store can be a great asset if you remember these guidelines.

2. Send a Clear Message That is Authentic to You

"To be a fashionable woman is to know yourself, know what you represent, and know what works for you. To be 'in fashion' could be a disaster on 90 percent of women. You are not a page out of Vogue."
—author unknown

Do you know who you are, what you stand for and how you expect to be treated? If you don't, it is going to be difficult for you to build an image that really works for you and furthers your goals.

Build a wardrobe out of basic and classic pieces with timeless appeal, and then spice things up with a few trendier items that can be edited out later. You will then have the makings of a wardrobe that will take you wherever you want to go for years to come.

Make a list of goals in different areas of your life. Try to come up with at least three. For example:

- Find a job making at least $80,000 per year.
- Have a more romantic relationship with my husband.
- Be a more authoritative, but fun, mom.

You get the idea. Now write down a few words that describe traits necessary to achieve these goals. Once you have an idea of the message you want to send, building an image to support that will be much easier. For instance, a high-paying professional position will require that you send forth a message of competence, dependability and leadership. One of the greatest tools at your disposal will be a matched suit, with additional coordinating pieces that allow you to mix and match. A jacket is always a sign of authority, and a matched suit is the height of professionalism. It is what the person in charge wears. In a formal work environment, use darker colors, firm fabrics with small or no pattern and straight or angular lines in the details and tailoring. This look says loudly, "I am in charge, I know what I am doing and I am worth every penny I am paid." Match this outfit with impeccable manners, and confident body language, and you will be seen by all as someone who is competent and confident.

A romantic look will use opposite cues, like softer, more playful colors, patterns that tend toward florals or other feminine themes and softer fabrics and curved lines, such as ruffles or flounces. Does this sound too soft for you? Never fear! Even a very assertive woman can wear a beautifully draped silk blouse and a string of pearls with a light-colored suit and look every bit the seductive woman. Know yourself, know your message and the battle is halfway won!

When at home, you can send the message that you are in charge and expect respect, even though you are wearing clothes that are appropriate to casual circumstances. Wearing jeans or khakis that are clean and pressed, either a shirt with a collar or a V-neck knit shirt with neatly styled hair and light makeup, clearly says you are in charge of your little world. The children can see you are ready for work or play, but are still the grown-up.

This is only a beginning of the many messages we send through our image. Be sure to consider what you want to say when preparing for the day.

3. Tailored, Not Tight!

"Those hot pants of hers were so . . . tight, I could hardly breathe!"
—Benny Hill, English comedian

Mr. Hill has discovered one of the great truths of life; if your clothing is so tight that you are having trouble breathing, men around you may have the same problem. The real issue is that tight clothing can be so distracting that people may never get past it to see who you really are.

There is nothing that will take a look from classy to cheap faster than clothing that is too tight or revealing. When thong underwear lines show through tight pants, when cellulite can be clearly seen through stretched fabric, when you have any visible color or texture showing through your bra and blouse, or if the men at the office stand in line to watch you—from either the front or the back—when you bend over the filing cabinet, you know that you are sending a message that yells "sex!" so loudly that the rest of what you say, verbally and visually, is not likely to be heard. Sex is such a powerful and basic part of our nature that it is always the 800-pound gorilla in the room. Sending a sexual message when you are looking for an intimate companion is one thing, but sending it—even subtly or unintentionally—when you are trying to relate to people non-sexually, is always a detriment. It is always noticed, even if people don't comment on it, and the attention is usually negative. I know a woman who was terribly offended when people at her job complained to the boss about her super-tight clothing. Though she does have the right to dress as she pleases, this ultra-tight look was causing problems with her co-workers and making it hard for them to see the wonderful woman behind the tight pants.

The hardest thing about this can be that we may not be aware we are sending that message. Perhaps the dress that was a perfect fit ten pounds ago now shows a lot more cleavage or thigh than it used to. Maybe a style that fashionably and modestly fits your thin friend looks like a Madonna-inspired stage ensemble on your curves. Even though the sexual message may be loud and clear to those around us, we may not see it so easily. Here are a few guidelines to help:

- One major key is ease. That means that the size of your garment should be from one inch to three inches larger than your body. This is actually a very small amount, and just means that you should be able to "pinch an inch" of fabric when wearing the piece. More than three inches may make it look too big, unless the specific style is intended to be loose, while a small amount of ease will make it look better-fitting. Another benefit of ease is that it makes you look slimmer since it floats lightly over the body contours instead of hanging up on every lump or bulge.

- Be sure that you have enough coverage at the neckline and hem. Give yourself a minimum one-inch safety margin. Check that you can get in and out of your car, bend over and sit down easily without exposed underclothing. By ignoring this simple rule, you can give away your credibility for a single inch! An inch of exposed cleavage that fastening one button could have covered, an inch of hemline that left everyone wondering what they were going to see when you crossed your legs, or an inch that made your blouse obviously strain over your bust, all send a message of sexuality that undermines the image you have worked so hard to achieve.

The Best Accessory of All

Several years ago, I read a funny article about responses little girls gave to questions about their mothers. My favorite was a little girl who, when asked the question, "Why did your mom marry your dad?" said, "Well, Grandma says she wasn't wearing her thinking cap!" While this is certainly funny, it also illustrates the point that it is wise to think before acting, and that we may not get what we really want if we forget to do that. So when you stand in front of your closet tomorrow morning, have the first accessory you choose be your thinking cap and ask yourself:

The Three Golden Questions of Image Management

1. What will I be doing today?

2. What message do I want to send?

3. How can I construct an image dynamically attractive to what I want?

As you read this book, I challenge you to be on the lookout for information that applies to your unique circumstances and goals. Write down things you want to try, research what you want to know more about and make a shopping list of items you want to add to your wardrobe. You will be learning about everything from how to use foundation garments to the correct application of makeup. You will discover why you look better physically—and feel better psychologically—in certain styles and what those styles communicate to others. You will learn about choosing hairstyles, using accessories, picking out eyeglass frames, shopping strategies, wardrobe building and more. Constructing your personal inspired style will be a wonderful adventure of learning and self-discovery, full of surprises and well—worth the effort. So as you begin, allow me to offer some inspirational words from the immortal fashion icon, Coco Chanel:

"I don't understand how a woman can leave the house without fixing herself up a little—if only out of politeness. And then, you never know, maybe that's the day she has a date with destiny. And it's best to be as pretty as possible for destiny."

Now go out with confidence and meet yours!

CHERYL OBERMILLER
Classic Image Consulting

Changing lives one closet at a time!

(816) 215-2313
cheryl@classicimageconsulting.com
www.classicimageconsulting.com

A former model and owner of Models by Cj, mother to a blended family of eight children, and the founder and owner of Obermiller Construction Services, a heavy construction company, Cheryl brings a colorful and diverse background to her career as an image management consultant, author and public speaker. Her professional experience in the fashion industry, combined with 16 years as president of Obermiller Construction Services, gives Cheryl a unique and practical approach to image consulting.

> *"What 98-pound models are wearing in Paris has little to do with the kind of image information most women can really use. The average woman needs to be able to go to her closet in the morning and quickly pull together an attractive look that tells the world who she is, what she stands for and exactly how she expects to be treated."*

With a passionate commitment to helping women understand how they can use their image as a tool to improve their relationships, further their careers, reach their goals and skyrocket their self-esteem, Cheryl is committed to teaching women from all walks of life the hows and the whys of personal image.

Love Your Body, Love Your *Life!*
A Guide to Positive Body Image and a Great Life

By Oreet Mizrahi, AICI FLC

*H*ow many times have you looked in a mirror and thought: "If only...?" "If only I could increase/decrease/erase/replace this or that part of my body, then I could really love my body and be pleased with the way I look."

As a body image specialist and image consultant, I can tell you that the vast majority of my clients live with this inner dissatisfaction and self-criticism. It should not be this way. If you want to enhance your look and be able to project your best image, you need to choose to love your body. You must accept your body the way it is right now, and go out of your way to give it love and tender care.

Looking good and feeling good about your body is an internal experience, an inside awareness as well as a practiced skill. There is a powerful connection between your body, your mind, your spirit and the way you look and feel. The image you project to the world and the way others see you all have to do with the way you perceive yourself and the body image you hold. As a matter of fact, looking good and feeling good about your body has nothing to do with your shape or size. Rather, it comes from body talk, self-talk, messages, beliefs and habits. It is all about developing a positive body image and knowing

11

how to love your body. Once you learn to love your body, your self-confidence will soar, you will feel energetic and happy and you will be able to live your best life.

"Someone's opinion of you does not have to become your reality."
—Les Brown, American motivational speaker

Invent a New Fashion Trend

Express your own version of attractiveness and dare to look different. Actually, looking different and projecting your individuality can be very stylish. Let your unique beauty shine by creating your own version of beauty. Decide to become the specialist of your own body. You need not try to live up to someone else's ideal, or to follow any fashion trend. Most of us will never look like supermodels, no matter how little we eat or how much we exercise. Furthermore, beauty standards are forever changing; what is considered a perfect body today may not be perceived as such in 20 years or so. Marilyn Monroe, an ultimate beauty symbol, was a size 12. According to current beauty values, she would have been considered overweight and flabby. Imagine that!

Do you really want to spend your life criticizing and fighting your body? Accept yourself and love your body just the way it is right now! Start with determining what your personal ideal body weight should be. Remember that one person's ideal body weight is different than another's, so set realistic expectations.

How to Determine Your Personal Ideal Body Weight

No charts, measurements or formulas can really tell you your ideal body weight. Don't rely on the scale, either—weighing yourself is the last thing you want to do. The numbers on the scale are just numbers.

They say nothing about how good you look. Actually, it is not even an indication of how healthy you are.

Your ideal body weight is the weight that allows you to feel fit, strong and energetic. At your ideal weight, you are able to lead a healthy, normal life. You are not tired, frustrated, anxious or angry. You have the energy to participate in sports, concentrate on your work, and maintain a healthy relationship with family and friends. No one can decide for you what is right and what looks good. This is an important thing to keep in mind. So create a new beauty trend. Challenge the era. Make your own fashion statement. Love your body, and just let your body be.

> *"If you can't get a compliment any other way, pay yourself one."*
> —Mark Twain, American author

Sweeten the Talk

Always use positive language and have encouraging thoughts and feelings toward your body. Listen to your inner talk and be well aware of the little voice inside your head. Are you saying nice things to yourself? Are you grateful for your body? Consider the marvelous functions of your body and its incredible worth. Replace negative feelings with respect and appreciation. Give yourself a compliment. By emphasizing all the great things your body does for you and by using words of praise, you shift from feelings of criticism and hate to feelings of love and appreciation. For instance, by saying to yourself, "My body is strong, beautiful and healthy," you start feeling positive about your body and soon you start to believe in what you are saying.

Positive affirmations are another powerful technique for learning to love your body. Post positive affirmations everywhere. This will help raise your self-esteem and will make it easier to appreciate and value your body. For instance, say this to yourself: "I love and accept myself completely and unconditionally." Read your affirmations out loud several times a day. Write them down and keep saying them to yourself. Soon, it will become your reality. Continue with that until you start feeling love for your body.

> *"Too many people overvalue what they are not*
> *and undervalue what they are."*
> —Malcolm Forbes, American publisher

Change Your Focus

How many times have you looked at yourself and overanalyzed and criticized your body parts? Don't do that! Instead of focusing on the parts of your body that you dislike, focus on the parts that you do like. Become aware of the gifts you have. Choose to focus on your positive features and pamper and emphasize the parts you love the most. Ask yourself what body parts you do like. From my experience with my clients, this is not an easy thing to do. Most of us are so used to judging our bodies and finding flaws that we completely forget to notice our blessings.

Try the following exercise: Take a minute and close your eyes. Think of the different parts of your body. Focus on one part of your body that you really like. For example, think of the sparkle in your eyes, or remember your beautifully shaped legs or your lovely hands. Find all the things that are right with your body. Do this until you feel a positive shift in your mood. Open your eyes and write down as many favorite body parts as possible. Choose to shift your focus and concentrate on them. Become aware of the qualities you have and be proud of them. Learn how to play them up and show them off. For example, if you have a great pair of shapely legs, don't be afraid to show them in short skirts. Invest in a sparkly ankle bracelet or paint your toenails a bright, dazzling color. Looking good has nothing to do with being perfect. It is all a matter of being aware of your assets and knowing how to project and reveal them.

"Life is like riding a bicycle. To keep your balance you must keep moving."
—Albert Einstein, German-American physicist

Move Your Body

You can change the way you feel and look and dramatically improve the quality of your life just by keeping your body moving. Your body is your vehicle for experiencing the world and it is meant to be moving. Walking, running and jumping are all natural and essential to the body. Have you ever seen a still, unmoving body of water? The sight can be appalling. Still water is stagnant, sluggish and polluted. Guess what? Your body is approximately sixty percent water. Life and energy are in movement. Being active will make you look alive. Your skin will sparkle and your image will proclaim life.

Inactivity will make you lethargic, inefficient and dull-looking. To look good, feel good and live your best life, you must keep your body active. Make a commitment to move your body any way you like. Begin to practice moving and enjoy it so that you end up doing it on a regular basis. It doesn't matter what kind of exercise or sport you do. Walk, run, swim or garden. Dare to dance. Leap and jump. Your body was meant to be in motion, so keep it moving and use this special time to connect with your body. Don't exercise only to burn calories or to lose weight. Exercise to relax, to have fun and to connect with your body and with your surroundings.

Try to exercise outdoors while exploring nature. Take long walks with no other purpose than walking itself. Explore your environment. Use your senses to feel your body and to enjoy life. See the sights. Smell the scents. Listen to the beauty of creation. Feel the fresh air on your face. Take deep breaths. Feel revitalizing energy fill your body. This is what exercising is all about.

> *"Love yourself, for if you don't, how can you expect anybody else to love you?"*
> —Susan Lipsett and Liz Nelson, authors

Boost Your Self-Confidence

Someone once said that low self-esteem is like driving through life with the hand-brake on. To look your best, you first need to practice self-love and to boost your self-esteem. People who love their life are usually people who have a strong sense of self-worth. Treat yourself with respect. Take care of your body and treat it as you would treat a best friend. Always get yourself top quality. Surround yourself with flowers. Cook a tasty meal. Set the table with your best china and use the finest silverware. Put on your best lingerie. Sleep on luxury linen. Feed your body nourishing food. Eat when you are hungry, and stop when full. Know that you deserve the best. Don't deprive yourself of anything.

Be good to yourself and love your body. You need to learn to be better to yourself in order to expect better from life and from the universe. The universe can only match your vibrations. This is the law of attraction. Everything you focus on and put emotional energy on will eventually be attracted into your life. Your thoughts and feelings create your reality. The universe and your subconscious cannot tell the difference between beliefs and actuality. You can't disrespect your body or hate yourself and expect the universe to send love and blessings into your life. The universe can only match your vibrations. When you take good care of yourself, treat your body with respect, and know your self-worth, the universe will respond accordingly.

I have a very powerful exercise to boost your self-confidence called the "Mirror Exercise." This is a great exercise that delivers significant results. As simple as it might sound, you will find it extremely difficult to do at first. Don't give up. Like any new skill, the more you practice it, the better you will become. Find some private time and stand in front of a mirror. Look in the mirror and tell yourself how much you love your body. State your name and look deep into your own eyes. Say words of appreciation and gratitude to your body. Thank your body for all the great things it does for you. Clear your mind of judgments and let negative feelings fade away. You might feel awkward and embarrassed at first, but don't turn away from your reflection. Now look closely at those parts you resist the most. Most of us judge each of our body parts individually. Send love and affection toward them. Try experiencing your body as a whole and not as a collection of separate parts that need improvement. Practice the mirror exercise at least twice a day. Keep doing it and one day you will be able to look at your body and feel pure love and admiration.

> *". . . do ordinary things in an extraordinary way."*
> —Arthur P. Stanley, English clergyman and author

Love Your Body with All Your Senses

Imagine how pleasurable your life would be if you could love your body with all five senses. Stimulate your senses and use them to feel pleasure and enjoyment. Find out what sights, smells, sounds, touch and tastes fuel your soul. Become aware of your surroundings and notice the things around you that inspire and encourage you. What is it that awakens your motivation? What stirs your emotions? What is it that arouses your attention? You deserve to live in an atmosphere of joy and you ought to be able to feel pleasure. Our senses are powerful tools that can change our experience completely, yet we often neglect to take advantage of them and experience pleasure for ourselves.

Stimulate your sense of sight by surrounding yourself with beautiful things. Take a moment and look around you. Find things that please your eyes and awaken your sense of aesthetics; get a manicure and paint your nails a beautiful color, surround yourself with flowers. Know which colors look good on you and choose your clothes and makeup accordingly. Eat your food slowly and enjoy every bite. Let the tastes melt on your tongue and fill your mouth with flavor. Choose to be in control of the sounds around you. Play wonderful music that lifts your spirit. Don't let electronic devices dominate your life. Be aware and eliminate negative noise. Spend time outdoors and be attuned to the sounds of nature.

Did you ever notice how different smells can change your feelings? Calming lavender and sage are great ways to relax your mind and body. For a playful atmosphere, try peppery fragrances. For a seductive feel, wear spicy scents.

Touch and beauty are correlated on many levels. Hands-on treatments such as massages, facials or pedicures are fantastic ways to boost your mood. Did you know that the human touch releases endorphins that can help reduce stress and anxiety? Psychologically, touch can also make you feel less lonely and more protected. Wear clothes that are comfortable and pleasant to the touch. Take a warm bath with essential oils. The options are endless. Go with your imagination. Dream big and indulge your body.

Twenty More Ways to Love Your Body and Live Your Best Life:

- Think gorgeous

- Bring nature into your body and into your life

- Smile, smile, smile!

- Choose to wear clothes that give you comfort, energy and style

- Invest time and money in finding the right bra

- Don't compare yourself to others

- Dare to dance

- Sing out loud!

- Drink plenty of water

- Dare to be different

- Take beauty breaths

- Strike a pose

- Dry brush your body

- Conceal your imperfections

- Reveal and emphasize your assets

- Always buy first class and top quality. Always!

- Fall in love with yourself

- Schedule a special "me time" every day

- Change your goal from weight loss to health gain

- When everything else fails, wear a hat, hold your head up and put on a smile…

You will look fantastic!

*"You yourself, as much as anybody in the entire universe deserve
your love and affection."*
—Buddha, founder of the Buddhist religion

Commit to love your body! Not only will you look good, you will feel
amazing. Taking care of yourself from the inside helps you enhance
and improve your outside. Feeling good and looking good go hand in
hand. This is what beauty is all about; looking your best means feeling
good and comfortable in your own skin. You only have one body and
one life. Make sure to fill them both with love. Love your body today;
love your life forever. If *you* won't do it, who will?

OREET MIZRAHI, AICI FLC
Body Image & Appearance Expert

Expressing Excellence,
Confidence & Style

(561) 789-1313
oreet@mizrahiimage.com
www.mizrahiimage.com

*O*reet Mizrahi is the owner and president of Oreet Mizrahi International Image Consultant. As a body image and appearance expert, with a profound understanding of principles of proportion, style, wardrobe needs and body language, it is easy to see how Oreet rapidly earned a worldwide reputation. Although Oreet is familiar with many aspects of image consultancy, her passion lies with body image and body language awareness. Developing awareness and a positive relationship with one's own body and being able to recognize and understand its language is fundamental for establishing a strong sense of self-confidence and an elevated self-esteem. Improving body awareness will result in feeling good about the way one looks, which Oreet finds tremendously satisfying.

Specializing in the areas of semiotics—signs and symbols in nonverbal communication—appearance and body image, Oreet is an international certified image consultant and a certified self-esteem coach. Oreet deems that the all-important "good first impression," coupled with a commanding, constant presence, is definitely the key to personal and professional success. Residing in Parkland, Florida, with her husband and their four children, Oreet's goal is to live life with passion!

The Yin and Yang *of* Style

By Pat Gray, PhD, AICI FLC

"I am the feminine.
I am the masculine.
I am one and I am both.
My darkness can be trying.
My lightness can be blinding.
But in balance there is harmony."
—Peter Sanderson, French-American poet

*W*hat does the concept of yin yang have to do with style? By knowing our combination of yin yang characteristics, we can achieve harmony and balance in our outer appearance by choosing clothing that integrates our yin and our yang traits. In doing this, our psyche is satisfied and we feel confident, happy and in control. Our outer appearance is no longer a top concern, and we can turn our energies to our other endeavors. We can also use our knowledge of yin and yang to further our work and life goals by sending the appropriate unspoken messages through our clothing choices.

Traditional Yin Yang

The concept of yin and yang comes from ancient China. It is a way of describing two opposite, but complementary, principles or forces.

Yin is usually seen as the darker, less energetic side and yang as the brighter, more energetic side. Here is a comparison of yin and yang in the ancient Chinese way.

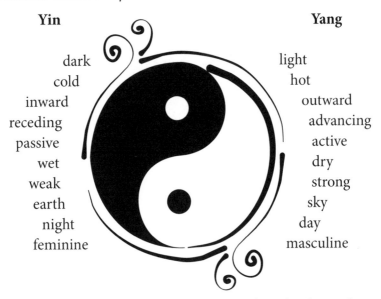

Yin	Yang
dark	light
cold	hot
inward	outward
receding	advancing
passive	active
wet	dry
weak	strong
earth	sky
night	day
feminine	masculine

These two forces—yin and yang—interact with each other to form the whole. It is a duality that results in a unity. You cannot have yin without yang, dark without light, earth without the sky. This can be seen in the symbol for yin yang. One cannot be without the other; and one flows into the other.

Now let's look at the concept of yin and yang in terms used by image consultants to describe a person's physical, psychological, and clothing characteristics.

Physical and Psychological Yin Yang Characteristics

In 1936, Belle Northrup published a paper entitled "An Approach to the Problem of Costume and Personality" in the annual *Art Education Today*, published by the Bureau of Publications, Teachers College of Columbia University. She used this concept of yin yang to describe a person's physical and psychological traits and to describe clothing and clothing design elements. In 1956, Harriet T. McJimsey expanded Northrup's work as *Costume Selection,* published by Burgess Publishing, as well as in two later works. Judith Rasband adapted and expanded the yin yang concepts in 1975 as *Clothing Style Selection,* published by the Brigham Young University Press; and again in 1996 within Wardrobe Strategies for Women, published by Delmar. Rasband expanded the yin yang concepts to include menswear in *Personal Style,* published by the Conselle Institute of Image Management in 1998.

What are some physical characteristics of yin and yang?

Yin	Yang
Small bone structure	Large bone structure
Light weight	Heavy weight
Light skin	Dark skin
Blue eyes	Brown eyes
Blonde	Brunette
Rounded body shape	Straight body shape
Short	Tall
Small facial features	Large facial features
Rounded facial features	Angular facial features
Curly hair	Severe hairstyle
Youthful	Mature
Weak	Strong
Low contrast	High contrast
Soft voice	Loud voice
High-pitched voice	Low-pitched voice
Smooth skin	Coarse skin
Graceful gait	Purposeful gait

It is important to note that we are rarely strictly all yin or all yang. We are a combination of yin and yang. An individual may be very yin in one trait, very yang in a second, and somewhere on the continuum between yin and yang in a third trait.

Let's look at some well-known celebrities who characterize yin and yang. Cher is a typical yang. She is tall, dark, angular, has high contrast and has large facial features. At the other end is Grace Kelly. She is fair, low contrast, rounded and youthful. She is a typical yin.

Let's take a look at some real-life women. Susan is large, tall and dark. These are very yang characteristics. But she is curvy, a yin characteristic. She also has moderately-sized facial features which places her somewhere between yin and yang. Dolores is short, small, blonde and light—all yin characteristics. Her dark brown eyes are a yang characteristic. These examples show how one person can have some yin characteristics, some yang characteristics and some characteristics that are midway between yin and yang.

Take some time now to determine your combination of yin yang physical traits. Circle the traits in the chart on the previous page that best describe you. If you are in between on a characteristic, place an "X" between the two traits. Are you mostly yin, mostly yang or a combination of both yin and yang? Are you in between on some characteristics? Knowing yourself makes it much easier to choose your most appropriate clothing styles.

Now let's examine some psychological characteristics.

Yin		Yang
Friendly		Reserved
Warm		Cool
Dependent		Independent
Introverted		Extraverted
Quiet	✓	Loud
Timid	✓	Bold
Innocent		Sophisticated
Dainty	✓	Firm
Compliant	✓	Resistant
Flexible		Unyielding
Emotional		Unemotional
Indirect	✓	Blunt
Impractical		Practical
Gentle		Rough
Easygoing		Temperamental
Gracious		Abrupt

Our celebrities—Cher and Grace Kelly—have psychological yin yang characteristics that match their physical yin yang characteristics. Cher is bold and sophisticated. Grace Kelly is ladylike and gracious.

Analyze your psychological yin yang traits by circling which adjectives best describes you. Again, if you are in between on a characteristic, place an "X" between the two traits. Are you mostly yin, mostly yang, a combination of the two or in between on some characteristics?

Overall, do your physical yin yang traits match your psychological yin yang traits or not? If your physical and psychological traits complement each other, then it is much easier to choose clothing styles. But if you are more yin in one and more yang in another, it will take more thought to have your clothing harmonize with both your physical and psychological selves.

Yin Yang Clothing Characteristics

Now that you have some idea of your yin yang physical and psychological characteristics, let's look at how this relates to clothing design elements and styles.

Yang style clothing can be described best as tailored, dramatic, sophisticated and mature. Design elements seen in yang clothing are:

- Straight lines
- Long lines
- Unbroken lines
- Angular shapes
- Dark value colors
- Bright colors
- Black and white
- High contrast
- Firm, woven, smooth fabrics
- Opaque fabrics
- Large scale
- Large, abstract or geometric prints
- Few details

Examples of clothing and accessories that a yang person would wear are capes, swing coats, leggings, long sweaters, high heels, statement necklaces, high boots, long coats, peaked lapels, cuff bracelets, large scarves and shawls.

Yin style clothing can be described as untailored, feminine, soft and dressy. Design elements seen in yin clothing are:

• Curved lines

• Broken lines

• Rounded shapes

• Light colors

• Muted colors

• Low contrast

• Soft fabrics that drape well

• Sheer, transparent fabrics

• Small scale

• Many details

Examples of clothing and accessories that a yin person would wear are puff sleeves, pleated or gathered skirts, lacy blouses, ruffled blouses, rounded collars, Mary Jane shoes, pearls, floral prints, silk scarves, slingback shoes, strappy shoes and vintage jewelry.

Here are a few quick questions you can ask yourself to help determine your preferences for yin or yang clothing. When you pick out your outfit for the day, do you immediately think of which belt you'll wear with it? Or do you think about which earrings to wear? When you go shopping, are you always looking for the perfect shoes? Or do you look for that fabulous scarf? Yang style clothing emphasizes the waist and hemline. So if you like to accessorize with shoes and belts, you have a preference for yang clothing. Yin style clothing emphasizes the neckline. So if you prefer accessorizing with earrings and a scarf around your neck, you have a preference for yin clothing styles.

A Continuum of Yin and Yang

Most likely, when you analyzed your yin and yang characteristics, you were not all yin or all yang. How do you dress if you have some yin and some yang characteristics? What if you're in between the continuum of yin and yang? Belle Northrup's paper described six categories of personal style. These six styles were later updated by Rasband and included styles for men in every category except Delicate.

Northrup	Rasband
Ingénue	Delicate
Gamin	Sporty
Romantic	Romantic
Classic	Classic
Athletic	Sportive
Dramatic	Dramatic

These styles form a continuum between yin and yang. Ingénue/Delicate and Gamin/Sporty are the most untailored and most yin, Romantic and Classic are between untailored yin and tailored yang, and Athletic/Sportive and Dramatic are the most tailored and most yang. This continuum encompasses physical characteristics, psychological characteristics and clothing styles. In order to understand this, let's look at a few yin and yang characteristics and how they fit into this clothing system.

Ingénue/Delicate and Sporty people are short, usually below average in height. Romantic and Classic people are of average height.

Athletic/Sportive and Dramatic types are tall and above average in height.

Women with Ingénue/Delicate, Sporty or Romantic styles are the most submissive, with the Ingénue extremely submissive and the Romantic less so. Women with Classic, Athletic/Sportive or Dramatic styles are the most assertive. A woman with Dramatic style might be so assertive as to seem aggressive or intimidating, while a woman with a Classic style might be seen as assertive yet gracious.

Clothing styles will also fall onto a continuum between the yin Ingénue and the yang Dramatic. An Ingénue might wear a dressy dress, a Romantic a softly tailored dress and a Sportive a tailored menswear suit. This shows the gradual transition from yin to a combination of yin and yang to mostly yang.

Another transition from yin to yang is seen with the Ingénue style, characterized by all-over floral prints, moving to the traditional paisley prints of the Classic style, and on to the large abstract or animal prints of the Dramatic style.

"Know yourself first, and then adorn yourself accordingly."
—Epictetus, Greek philosopher

It is impossible in this short chapter to give enough information for you to determine exactly which style you fall under. However, you should be able to determine if you fall mostly in the yin categories, mostly in the yang categories or in between. Your image consultant can help you find your style using this system or others that have been developed in recent years. See Sally Templeton's chapter, *Develop Your Personal Style,* on page 47, for some possibilities about what styles are best for you.

Now would be a good time to look over your yin yang characteristics and determine where you fall on the continuum. Then review your wardrobe and decide where it lies on the continuum. Most likely, just like you, your wardrobe contains garments with both yin and yang characteristics. But is it mostly yin, mostly yang or some combination?

Is your wardrobe in balance with your physical and psychological yin yang characteristics? If it is, then your wardrobe is in great shape. Let's look at one person whose wardrobe is not in harmony with her characteristics.

Kim has many yin characteristics, both physical and psychological. She is slight, blond and soft-spoken. But because she works as a bank manager, she wears tailored suits to work. Her wardrobe has yang characteristics. What can she do to bring her wardrobe more into harmony with her characteristics? She can add a few yin designs, maybe a light-colored silk blouse with pearl buttons. The light color maintains high contrast (yang), but the silk and pearl buttons add some yin characteristics. Or she could add a large-scale (yang) floral (yin) brooch. Either of these would soften her overall effect but still maintain her professional look.

What if you are yin in psychological characteristics but yang in physical characteristics, or the reverse? How do you balance your wardrobe? That will take a little more thought. Robin has yin physical characteristics. She is curvy, low contrast and short. But she has yang psychological characteristics. She is extraverted, independent and sophisticated. She prefers to wear dresses, which is a yin dressing style. She can add some yang characteristics by looking for dresses in a dark color, with large-scale prints or with more straight lines than rounded lines.

Varying Your Yin Yang Mix to Match Your Moods and Roles

Clothing sends unspoken messages both to ourselves and to others around us. Yang style clothing sends the message that the wearer is professional, authoritative, formal, bold and sophisticated. Yin style clothing sends the message that the wearer is receptive, informal, friendly and warm.

"Independence, assurance, originality, self-control and refinement should all be visible in the cut of his clothes."
—Ellen Moers, American author

You can use this information to match your clothing to your moods and roles. If you are in a career such as banking or law, where it is important to look professional and responsible, you can skew your clothing more toward the yang. That doesn't mean you should dress as a Dramatic if your characteristics place you more as a Classic. Just wear your most yang outfits to work or add a few yang features to your business clothing.

If you are in a health care profession that does not require a uniform, such as speech therapy or psychotherapy, or if you are a child care provider, you may want to wear a few yin characteristics in your clothing—perhaps softer colors or less angular shapes. This will help you look approachable, friendly and supportive. People will be more comfortable in your presence and more likely to trust you with their care.

These unspoken messages are not found only in our careers. When you are home with your young children, you will probably wear softer, less tailored clothing. Also, you will probably wear softer, more yin-like clothing when with friends and family. And, you will definitely want to wear yin clothing when dating or out with your spouse. This does not mean you would go completely yin if your characteristics are mostly yang. A woman who is mostly yang and wears highly tailored, professional clothes for work may wear tailored trousers and a sweater, rather than a flowing skirt and lacy blouse, for leisure time.

> *"Don't be into trends. Don't make fashion own you, but you decide what you are, what you want to express by the way you dress and the way to live."*
> —Gianni Versace, Italian fashion designer

Now that you've had time to know yourself by looking at your yin yang characteristics, you'll be able to make educated clothing choices. You can now have your clothing be in harmony with who you are and what you do. And when you look good, you feel good, and you're ready to do good things.

PAT GRAY, PhD, AICI FLC
Pat Gray in Color Image Consulting

Live your life in harmony

(510) 593-8805
pat@patgrayincolor.com
www.patgrayincolor.com

*P*at received her PhD in biochemistry in 1980. After discovering that she did not like research, she moved her career into marketing. After 13 years as a stay-at-home mom, she moved into direct sales, first with Weekenders USA and later with Mary Kay Inc. She decided that she could better help her clients by knowing more about color.

While taking classes at Colour Designers International (CDI), she discovered her love and talent for color and style analysis. She is a Color Specialist member of CDI and a certified Universal Style consultant. Pat is a member of the Association of Image Consultants International and Treasurer of the San Francisco Bay Area chapter. She specializes in color analysis, style consultation, wardrobe audits, skincare and makeup for individuals, as well as professional dress for individuals and small businesses.

Reinvent *Yourself*

A Guide to Finding Your New Purpose and Realigning Your Image

By Julie Maeder, AICI FLC

*I*t happens to most people at some point in their lives. I know the signs and symptoms intimately, because it happened to me. I woke up one day with a very strong "woman's intuition" kind of feeling that I was on the wrong path. Do you know that feeling? Like something is just not right and if you don't make a big change, you will most likely lose your mind entirely and waste the rest of your life! It's quite an alarming wake-up call, and one that should not be ignored.

You have either experienced this kind of life-changing event already and want to know how to make the most of it, or you are smart enough to know that one could be lurking right around the corner. But not to worry. Even though the notion of "being on the wrong path" may sound negative and scary, it is actually the perfect stimulus for beginning a wonderful, new chapter of your life. It is your chance to start over—not completely from scratch, but with all the wisdom and life lessons you've accumulated with every step you've already taken—good *and* bad. You have the golden opportunity to reinvent yourself!

The "Fork in the Road"

There are many reasons for that proverbial "fork in the road." For some, it is a major trauma like a divorce or the death of a spouse. For others, it is an exciting career change, a big promotion or even retirement. It can even be the wonderful decision to become a mother, or the day that we think will *never* come—when the last chick leaves the nest. There are also physical reasons for a metamorphosis, like a major weight loss or undergoing cancer treatment.

Sometimes the reasons for standing at that fork in the road are caused by our own choices or desires for something better—something more meaningful in our lives. But often it is thrust upon us by outside forces beyond our control, which can leave us feeling helpless. And while these are two very different types of scenarios, the techniques for recognizing and optimizing them are quite similar.

How to Know When It's Time for a Change

We all know that timing is everything. I'm a firm believer that things happen for a reason, exactly when they are supposed to happen. A certain amount of planning is necessary, but trusting your gut is critical. You can have your whole life planned out—the perfect spouse, the perfect career, the perfect children, the perfect home—and then one day, something changes. Something just feels wrong.

There is no scientific research to guide you to know when it's time to make a change. There is, however, a strong voice inside your head that *will* tell you if you are open to hearing it. Here's how it sounded to me:

"I've been in this same career for over 20 years . . . I could do this job with my eyes closed . . . I need to get out from behind this computer . . . if I have to design one more brochure, I'm going to scream!"

I think it was the word *scream* that really got my attention. I had reached my limit and it was as clear as the bomb icon on my Mac. I immediately began searching for alternative career choices.

Analyzing Your Options

As I pondered my own future, dozens of random thoughts and ideas came to me. I had seen something on television about Monica Lewinski designing handbags. I could design handbags. Or maybe shoes—I *love* shoes—they're so sculptural. Or I would be eating out and announce to my husband that I could be a food critic. I *love* food and I'm a decent writer. I would be good at that. Or better yet, a *traveling* food critic. I also love painting and photography. Can I make a living being an artist?

I didn't realize it, but my subconscious mind was making a list (albeit scattered) of all of my passions and pairing them with like professions. Needless to say, it was completely overwhelming. There was no method to my madness, and all I did was create more confusion than clarity. So in order to avoid my pitfalls, here is what I suggest you do:

- Make four columns on a sheet of paper. Write the word *Passions* at the top of the first column. In the column next to that, write the word *Career,* followed by *Training* and lastly, *Rate 1-10.*

- Begin by writing down as many of your passions in the first column as you can think of, leaving several spaces between each one. Try to remember back when you were in high school or college—what did you hope to do one day? Let your mind go free to explore anything and everything you ever loved. The sky is the limit!

- Next, get creative and think of as many career choices as possible to align with each passion. For example, if writing is your passion, career choices could be editor, author, copywriter, poet or lyricist. Do not rule anything out at this point.

- If you are not overflowing with ideas, I recommend reading *What Color Is Your Parachute? 2009: A Practical Manual for Job-Hunters and Career-Changers*, by Richard Nelson Bolles, published by Ten Speed Press. Another excellent book is *Now, Discover Your Strengths*, by Marcus Buckingham and Donald O. Clifton, published by The Free Press, 2001.

- Under *Training*, write down any additional education you will need to be able to perform that particular job. You might need to do some online research. There are plenty of websites that can help if you search under *career training*.

- Finally, rate your desire for each new career choice from 1 to 10.

Once your chart is completed, you will have a very clear, concise look at each and every option that appeals to your passions and strengths, as well as an idea of how easily you will be able to segue into that field. No more scattered thoughts and feeling overwhelmed. You will now have something tangible to help you make this wonderful decision.

To assist you in finding your dreams and passions, surround yourself with loving, supportive people. Avoid toxic people who will sap your physical and emotional energy. Be sure to take good care of yourself by eating well, exercising, meditating and getting enough sleep. This will keep your energy level up and your mind clear and focused.

As for me, the light bulb went on one day while I was reading an article in *More Magazine* about an image consultant in New York City. I had no idea these marvelous creatures existed outside of Hollywood or Washington D.C., and the realization that this was a viable career choice for a Midwestern girl such as myself thrilled me beyond belief! It encompassed so many of my passions: fashion, design and *shopping.* This was the beginning of my own exciting reinvention!

Of course, a career change is only one of many types of reinvention. I see my clients experiencing all sorts of shifts in their lives. Very often, it is a promotion at work. Take my client Catherine, for example. She used to be "behind the scenes" where she only came into contact with other employees. Suddenly, she found herself front and center—managing teams, giving presentations, taking clients to lunch and traveling for business. This was a whole new ball game, and she was wise enough to know that the casual sweaters and khakis she mindlessly threw on every morning would no longer cut it. She needed to reinvent her image to keep pace with her new role. It really is no different if you are a new mom, a new divorcee, or a new retiree. The process for metamorphosis is the same.

Adopting a Positive Attitude

One of the greatest keys to a successful reinvention is your attitude. A positive outlook is more important than any other single thing you can do for yourself. In fact, thinking positive thoughts releases endorphins and serotonin in the brain, which leads to increased happiness, satisfaction, energy and improved health! Even if the change you are experiencing is not of your own choosing, such as a divorce or the death of a spouse, you *can choose* how you react to it. Of course, you will grieve for your loss, but hopefully in time, you will realize that every ending really *is* a new beginning. If you can accept change as the only constant in life, then you can embrace the new road ahead.

Try to stay in the company of cheerful, positive people. This will go a long way in helping you maintain a great attitude. Make a conscious effort to look for the positive in every situation—it can be done! Avoid the constant stream of negative news in the media. Opt for inspiring books, CDs and videos instead. You'll be amazed at how these few simple things can impact your mental outlook.

Once you have gotten into the right frame of mind for this new chapter of your life, it's time to assess your current image. It might have served you well in the past, but you have moved on, and your image should always be a reflection of who you are *right now*.

Reviewing Your Wardrobe

Your clothes tell a unique story. What do they say about you? To find out, start by reviewing the clothes that are currently in your closet. Don't try to tackle your entire wardrobe all at once—just start with this season.

- With an objective eye, or the help of a friend, scan through your wardrobe as if you have never seen it before. Don't forget your accessories—shoes, handbags, scarves and jewelry. On a sheet of paper, write *Current Image* at the top. Below that, list at least six adjectives that describe the personality of your wardrobe as a whole. You might put down things like *conservative, predictable, drab, artistic, sensual* or *colorful.* The more adjectives, the better. This list will paint a picture of the image you have been projecting through your wardrobe.

- Below that list, write *New Image.* Now list six or more adjectives that are in alignment with your new, reinvented self. Are you more *independent, in control, casual, confident, calm, colorful* or *energized?* Whatever words come to mind quickly—write them down! You should have an immediate response to this for it to be truly authentic.

- Identify other women you admire who are also in your new role. What are some of their characteristics? If they spark excitement in you, write those words down in your *New Image* list.

- Now compare the two lists. Do you see a shift *away from* something and *toward* something else? This new list is going to be very important. It is the roadmap to your new image.

- Go back through your wardrobe, piece by piece. Examine each article to determine if it supports the adjectives in your *New Image* list. For example, if one of your new words is *energized,* put your drab, green sweater in a separate pile to be given to a charity or a resale shop. It will not feel right on you anymore, and it will not reflect the changes that have taken place within you. Do not settle for clothes that just look okay. On the other hand, if one of your new words is *creative* and you have a good, classic (but decidedly *un*creative) suit, hang onto it. You can add your own creative flair later with a unique blouse and accessories.

- Other criteria for editing your wardrobe: let go of anything you have not worn in a year or more, anything out-of-date, or just plain worn out. Also remove things that do not fit well or flatter you.

Rebuilding Your Wardrobe

After you have finished editing your closet, you can modify and build on what's left. Start with the basics. Do you have a good *core wardrobe,* or are there now some gaps to fill? A core wardrobe is comprised of essential pieces, including at least one suit, dress (one that can be dressed up or down like a little black dress), tailored jacket, slacks, skirt, shirt, shell, sweater, coat and a good pair of jeans. Core accessories include shoes, boots, a scarf, handbag, belt and jewelry. Invest in the best quality pieces you can reasonably afford.

- As you look through your closet, make a list of things you now need to fill in your wardrobe gaps. If this task feels a little daunting, I would encourage you to enlist the help of a local image consultant. You can find one in your area by going to www.aici.org or check the *More Inspired Style* section of this book on page 243 to see if any of the co-authors are in your area.

- Remember to take your *New Image* words and your shopping list when you head to the stores. As you shop, decide if each item supports your new adjectives. If not, step away from the rack! Don't settle for anything less than fantastic.

- Use the *core wardrobe* as a reference point, but always take your own lifestyle into account. If you are retired, for example, you may not need a suit. Build upon that core with items that represent your own individual personality. Adding a unique jacket and interesting jewelry to a basic shell and tailored slacks changes the look from traditional to artistic or dramatic. Mix and match things in unique and inspiring ways.

- Experiment with accessories to transform your attire. For more on that, see Dominique Vaughan-Russell's chapter, *Accessory Challenge!* on page 105. Also look for garments that complement your natural coloring. You can learn about this in Cynthia Lee Miller's chapter, *You Are More than Just a Season,* on page 59.

Time for a New 'Do

Many women get stuck in a grooming rut. They find a hairstyle they like and stick with it. Every year or two—and especially at a time like this—you should reassess your hairstyle and makeup. You can do the same exercise here as you did with your wardrobe:

- Write down six or more adjectives that describe your hair and makeup. It could be things like *sexy, sophisticated, sporty* or *casual.*

- Now compare this list to your *New Image* words. Are they in alignment? If not, look through magazines for pictures of hairstyles and makeup treatments that look more like your new words.

- Then consult with your hairstylist and perhaps a makeup artist, showing them the photos and discussing the effects you would like to achieve. Just be sure the look you want suits your facial shape and natural coloring.

You've come a long way, haven't you? You have found a new purpose. You have reinvented yourself, and your image now reflects the profound changes in your life. Congratulations! While this is no small task, you will reap the rewards every day as you go out into the world, confident that your outer appearance is in perfect harmony with the new person you have become.

JULIE MAEDER, AICI FLC
New Leaf Image Consulting

Your personal image mentor

(248) 457-9573
julie@newleafimageconsulting.com
www.newleafimageconsulting.com

*W*hen Julie discovered image consulting, she knew this would be the perfect segue from her 20-year career as an art director. She has blended her expertise in design and visual communication with her love of people and fashion into a harmonious reinvention of her creative skills.

Julie's passion for image consulting comes from the joy she feels in helping others feel great about themselves. Although she specializes in women in transition, Julie also transforms clients at all stages of life—from new graduates to moms, CEOs and retirees. Her role as image consultant is part detective, part fashion guru and part confidante. There is no "one-style-fits-all" approach—only a thoughtful exploration of who you are, where you want to be in your life, and how to help you get there.

Based in Troy, Michigan, Julie is a certified image consultant and member of the Association of Image Consultants International. She is a graduate of The University of Michigan with a bachelor's degree in Art and Design. Julie is currently serving on the Board of Directors for the Chicago Chapter of AICI as the VP of Marketing.

Develop *Your* Personal Style

By Sally Templeton

"Create your own visual style . . . let it be unique for yourself and yet identifiable for others."
—Orson Welles, American actor and director

First impressions count, and more than half of a first impression comes from how you look to others. Visual signals create lasting impressions that affect both personal and professional career opportunities. Your personal style is your individual look. It tells the world who you are and what you think about yourself. What you are inside is visible in your personal style.

Your personal style speaks louder than your words and is a powerful communication tool. Like most tools, you can use it to build something great, or it can be misused and put you in the position of having to repair a style mistake. Unfortunately, image mistakes can be hard to overcome. You have probably seen "What was she thinking?" photos where photographers have captured celebrities looking less than their best. You never want to be the "star" in that kind of photo!

What is "Personal Style?"

"To me style is just the outside of content, and content the inside of style, like the outside and the inside of the human body. Both go together, they can't be separated."
—Jean-Luc Godard, French/Swiss film director

Many things make up your personal style, including clothing, grooming, posture, gestures, energy levels and spirit. In order to create a personal style, you need to answer some questions:

How do you see yourself now?

• Do people see what you want them to see or is there a disconnect?

• What do you want to say to the world, friends, clients, boyfriend, husband and so on?

• Write a sentence or two that describes how you see yourself now.

Is anything holding you back from expressing yourself?

• Is it shyness?

• Is it "overwhelm?"

• Is it fear?

• Write a sentence or two about what holds you back. Is this something you can overcome? How?

What makes you unique?

• What are your best features?

• What do you want to enhance?

• What do you want to minimize?

• Write a sentence or two about how you can dress to focus attention on what is positive.

How to Create Your Personal Style

"I am very out of style . . . or I should say I have my own style."
—Alexandra Paul, American actress

Sometimes, it can be difficult to put a label on what your style is. Generally, most styles fall within a few basic categories. Designers describe styles in different ways; these are the five categories I use with my clients to help them focus on the image they want to achieve:

Dramatic. This style is bold and theatrical. It makes a statement about someone who is not afraid to stand out, who exudes confidence and is comfortable wearing bold colors and prints. Some designers known for their dramatic clothing are Versace, Gucci and Christian Dior.

Trendy. This style is for someone who follows current styles and trends. They are innovative and understand street fashion. Some designers known for creating trendy designs are Betsey Johnson, Dolce & Gabbana, Marc Jacobs and Dsquared[2].

Preppy. This is the country club style. It includes casual polos, button downs, plaids, argyles and walking shorts. Preppy designers are Ralph Lauren, Lacoste, Polo and Lilly.

Business formal. This is the classic, tailored, clean look in solid colors. Designers for this look include Giorgio Armani, Calvin Klein and Ann Taylor.

Business casual. This style includes comfortable, professional clothing with trouser pants, dressy jeans, buttoned-down and knit tops, sweater sets and dresses. Designers known for this style are Liz Claiborne, Isaac Mizrahi, Cynthia Taylor, The Gap and Banana Republic.

Which of the five styles are yours? You might have some of each. If you do, you might want to give some serious thought to your personal style and focus on one or two styles over the others. Mixing too many styles confuses people. They do not know who you are or what you represent.

Start to focus your style by going through magazines and collecting pictures of looks you like. A personal style will start to emerge. Create a file for shoes, dresses, handbags, haircuts, anything that appeals to you. Select overall looks you are drawn to. Make sure everything works together to create a cohesive statement.

Must-Haves for Any Style

"A woman is never sexier than when she is comfortable in her clothes."
—Vera Wang, American fashion designer

Regardless of what styles you choose, you need these must-have garments in your wardrobe, but you do not have to dress like a clone. I have some tips for modifying these basics for different styles.

Little Black Dress. The little black dress is all you need to make a great impression for any occasion.

Dramatic: Add jet black, multi-strand beads or jet jewelry, black fishnet hose and Christian Louboutin pumps with red soles.

Trendy: Accessorize with zebra shoes and a matching bag.

Preppy: Add brown and black argyle tights and close-toed, low-heeled shoes.

Business formal: Add a pearl necklace and stud earrings.

Business casual: Wear silver or gold jewelry in contemporary designs and ballet flats.

Incredible Silk Scarf. A silk scarf can be worn around the neck, the shoulders, the waist or the hips. It is a multi-purpose accessory.

Dramatic: Drape the scarf off the left shoulder and hold it with a pin or angle it on your waist like a sarong.

Trendy: Wrap it around your head like a bandana or tie it to your designer bag and let it hang.

Preppy: Wrap it around your ponytail or wear it like a headband.

Business formal: Wear it like an ascot.

Business casual: Use it like a belt. Run it through the belt tabs on your pants or tie it around your waist with a tunic or skirt.

Pearls. A pearl necklace adds richness and elegance to any outfit.

Dramatic: Choose large pearls or wear many layers of pearls and include colored pearls.

Trendy: Wear pearls, gold chains and crosses in many layers.

Preppy: Wear pearls under your shirt so the pearls peek out at the neck.

Business formal: Choose a choker or opera length necklace for a professional suit.

Business casual: Pearls can be too dressy for business casual. Choose smaller pearls or a single, good pearl on a thin chain.

Wool Crepe Skirt. Wool crepe molds to the body and has a timeless, elegant richness. It is an investment piece.

Dramatic: Choose a long, straight skirt with a high slit. Pair it with sexy sandals for evening and knee-high boots or a pump with textured hose for day.

Trendy: Choose a mini A-line skirt with a hemline ruffle. Wear it with an ankle boot.

Preppy: Go for a short skirt and flat ballerina shoes.

Business formal: Wear a straight skirt to the knee or just below the knee. Pair with a two-inch pump.

Business casual: Wear a straight skirt to the knee or just below the knee. Pair with a dark tight and flat shoe.

Good-fitting Jeans. Every woman needs a jean that hits all the right places in the right way. A designer jean can go from day to night just by changing your top and accessories.

Dramatic: Wear a black jean with metallic thread or a metallic fabric jean. Add a brightly colored top.

Trendy: Go for worn, torn, faded jeans with a peasant cotton shirt.

Preppy: Choose a CK jean with a button-down shirt.

Business formal: Choose a dark blue jean with a tailored cotton blouse and jacket.

Business casual: Wear Levi's with a knit top.

White Cotton Shirt. Nothing is more versatile, and it can be worn with any style!

Dramatic: Choose a wrap top with French cuffs.

Trendy: Wear an ethnic, peasant top with embroidery.

Preppy: Choose a white, pressed polo or cap sleeve shirt.

Business formal: Go for cotton, tailored with a ruffled front.

Business casual: Wear a cotton polo.

Textured Hose. Hosiery is an important way of making a statement and taking an outfit from ordinary to unique.

Dramatic: Fishnet or lace

Trendy: Striped or pinwheel flower textures

Preppy: Plaid or argyle tights

Business formal: Solid tights or herringbone prints

Business casual: Solid tights

Fitted Jacket. Dress it up; dress it down. This is a staple of every wardrobe and any style.

Dramatic: Go for a long, princess-cut jacket with topstitching.

Trendy: Choose a trench or safari jacket.

Preppy: Wear a blazer with an emblem on the jacket pocket.

Business formal: Choose a classic, three-button jacket and wear it buttoned.

Business casual: Go for a short, cropped jacket and leave it open.

Flat Front, Straight-leg Pants. Wear them for day, night and everything in between.

Dramatic: Choose a palazzo pant with a chain belt.

Trendy: Wear a straight-leg pant with an obi belt.

Preppy: Go for a plaid, straight-leg pant or Capris.

Business formal: Wear a traditional trouser.

Business casual: Go for a cotton trouser.

Boots. They were made for walking—and fashion statements!

Dramatic: Choose thigh-high, leather boots.

Trendy: Go for a high-heel suede ankle boot or a flat fur ski boot.

Preppy: Wear leather riding boots.

Business formal: Choose leather knee-high boots with two-inch heels.

Business casual: Go for flat short boots or flat knee-high boots.

Seven Quick Tips for Enhancing Your Style

> *"If at first you don't succeed, failure may be your style."*
> —Quentin Crisp, English writer

You do not need to reinvent your wardrobe or invest in expensive couture clothing to enhance your style. Here are seven tips to help you get started creating a personal style that works for you.

1. Use color to make a statement. Color and fashion trends are good to know, but it is what calls to you inside that counts. Just a pop of color makes everything look new and revived. Lift tailored gray pants by adding a lavender, rose or turquoise top and you change the whole impact of your outfit. Focus on colors that enhance your body and features. What colors call to you? Make sure you have at least one article of clothing in your closet or one accessory that sings that color.

2. Use black the right way. Everyone loves black; it is dark and mysterious. It slims and gives contrast to everything, but not everyone looks good in black. If black washes out your complexion, make sure you put a more complimentary color next to your face with a scarf or necklace. Choose midnight blue, dark gray or rich chocolate brown instead of black for the same style statement.

3. Give new life to what you already have. I have a top I designed over eight years ago and paired it with a new dramatic necklace that matches it perfectly. I have been stopped in the airport and complimented—not about my necklace but about my eight-year-old top! The necklace gave it a new life. Take inventory of your wardrobe and invest in one new piece that pops something you already have and makes it look brand new.

4. Mix and match fabrics and textures to add interest and make a statement. Fabric involves all the senses—sight, sound, smell and touch. Think about the smell of leather, the sound of beads and fringe moving, the touch of silk and satin on your skin. Using a printed satin lining inside a business jacket is a special surprise. Mix leather and lace, suede and wool plaid, silk and feathers. Go through your closet and drawers and play. See what mixes and matches to create a new look.

5. Use accessories to bring out the real you. Unique pieces will set you apart and bring out your individuality. Jewelry can be dramatic and exciting. Consider cuff bracelets in gold or sliver with colored stones. Jet beads and pearls in all colors. A scarf or shawl can renew a suit. Start shopping at craft shows and add a few high-quality, one-of-a-kind accessories to your wardrobe.

6. Buy one well-made, must-have investment piece that will last a lifetime. Cheap chic rarely lasts beyond the season, so use these garments and accessories to add a current vibe to your image. Go slowly and start small. Add one good piece each season.

7. Draw attention to your best features. V-neck tops and U-shaped necklines lift your bust and focus the eye on your face. Add a dramatic necklace to make a statement. Play with different necklines and silhouettes to see what works best for you.

"Accent your positive and delete your negative."
—Donna Karan, American fashion designer

Once you have decided on the style or combination of styles you want, go through your closet and have fun. Mix and match garments, fabrics and accessories and create entirely new looks that capture the image you want. Some garments may no longer work for the style you are looking for. If so, give that clothing away or sell it.

Start a list of what you need to add or replace to take your wardrobe to the next level. Carry your list with you and focus on the style you want to communicate when you shop for clothing and accessories. Begin to make new choices that enhance your style. Before long, you will have transformed your wardrobe into something that truly expresses who you are.

SALLY TEMPLETON
Sally T Designs

Image rules!

1-888-4SALLYT
sally@sallytdesigns.com
www.sallytdesigns.com

*S*ally Templeton has more than 18 years of experience in uniquely and completely transforming the images of her clients. Her company, Sally T Designs, is a multi-faceted design group that helps both men and women create a personal fashion brand.

Sally matches the personality of her clients with contemporary styles to create a fabulous—and lasting—impression. Her creative clothing designs, makeup mastery and distinctive jewelry set her clients apart and make a bold statement about their fashion sense and style. Clients come from all occupations and lifestyles. Brides and grooms, fashion models, newcomers and established business executives, baby boomers, Gen Xers and Ys have all benefited from her knowledge and expertise.

Sally has an Associate Degree in Fashion Design from Houston Community College. She has taught fashion at Houston Community College and serves on the College's advisory board. She received the Rising Star Award from Fashion Group International, Houston Chapter. Sally gives her clients her full attention to understand their needs and meet their expectations.

You Are More *than* Just a Season
Use Color to Enhance Your Image and Your Life

By Cynthia Lee Miller, AICI FLC

*"I found I could say things with color and shapes
that I couldn't say any other way—things I had no words for."*
—Georgia O'Keeffe, American artist

There is one woman in every crowd; she captures absolute attention with her look. All eyes stop when they scan the room and focus on her. She radiates her own signature style—her canvas that she has adorned with items perfect for her. Her signature style speaks of who she is because she dresses with her own personal energies, personal intention and personal coloring in mind. You can be "that woman."

When you have a signature style, you show the "who" of who you are; and when that happens, you express your inner beauty. Your signature style is your first expression of who you are to those you meet.

You position yourself to turn heads with your signature style. This is not about purchasing clothing, or shopping or spending a great deal of money and time. It is about blending your personal energies, personal intention and who you are. It is based on your custom colors, fabric design suited to your personality and the resonant stylistic look you choose for yourself. When you think signature style; think color, design, look, intent!

59

One of the major components of signature style is your personal custom color—the color that brings an instant reaction of joy from you each time you see it. It is a complimentary color as it comes from your custom color palette and your emotional relationship with the color. I use my custom color on my business cards, in my decorating and in the clothing I wear. It becomes the "Rembrandt" of your wardrobe colors and is your formula for presenting your inner beauty outwardly.

What color turns you on, sparks enthusiasm from you and "fits" you more than all others? Red? Baby blue? Fuchsia pink? Select your custom color. Embrace it, love it and use it!

How We Create Your Custom Color Palette

According to Donna Cognac, AICI CIP, "An understanding of the impact of clothing color on one's complexion is not new. Color analysis is neither fad nor fallacy. It is a process by which we arrive at the color harmony that shows us in the most positive light. The well-trained color consultant brings this knowledge to her clients and changes their lives forever."

I cannot say enough about custom color charting (a type of individualized color analysis), which I find to be very exciting for each person who takes the time to claim their own color palette. Armed with your own personal individual colorings, you are able to build a wardrobe that reflects positive energy. Color captures, excites, radiates and speaks with its own voice. Trust in it, use it and be the best you can be.

Custom color charting provides a personalized, one-on-one review of your own individual colorings. Colors are actually hand-selected for your precise eye, hair, skin and blush colorations. These are matched to master shades to create your own personal custom color palette which precisely reflects your color image.

Custom color goes yet another step in creating an individualized, hand-selected color palette, allowing for precise identification of your ideal colors for every facet of fashion. This approach recognizes that you, like the proverbial snowflake, are a unique individual.

The Power and Energy of Color

"Colors, like features, follow the changes of the emotions."
—Pablo Picasso, Spanish artist

Color is the first thing you see and the last thing you forget. It surrounds us in nature, is the creative force in art and is ever present in fashion. Color enriches our lives.

Color communicates power and energy, inspires you and helps define who you are. It speaks volumes about how you feel about yourself and how you view your place in the world. You can enhance your sense of purpose and ability to attract what you want in life through your appearance—and color is the most important part of that.

Color is the quickest, most cost-effective way to be "in trend" each season. The right color can make an outfit, enhance your facial tone and transform your appearance. Adding a deeper understanding of color encourages new possibilities. Using color to communicate is an art you can learn.

Color affects your deepest self. Psychology tells us that color can change your vibration, mood and behavior. Advertisers, marketers and retail stores use color to send messages that draw people to what they are selling. Color incites action.

Advanced Color Analysis Is More than a Season

"The best color in the whole world is the one that looks good on you."
—Coco Chanel, French fashion designer

In the 1970 to 1980s, simplified seasonal color analysis became a popular approach for women who wanted to identify and use personalized color palettes in their wardrobe shopping. As I provided this service to my clients, I saw them become excited about discovering where they fit in the world of personal color. Seasonal color analysis gave many women a new appreciation for using color to compliment their outward appearance, provided a rough but functional color palette and offered knowledge about choosing and using colors.

Some women saw this trendy analysis as too simplistic, while others have allowed their season to last a lifetime. If you still use a color palette based solely upon your "season," it is time to re-evaluate your color palette and personal style. It is time to appreciate the impact of color on your life with a new depth of understanding. Your color design is yours alone. There is no other like it and it can evolve, with a fresh selection of colors that work best for you, just as your life evolves and changes.

According to Judith Rasband, author of *Wardrobe Strategies*, published in 2002 by Fairchild Publications, Inc., "You need to know that personal coloring changes during your life due to age, diet, exposure to the environment and health. Your color preferences also change as you mature, as you acquire new experiences and make changes in your goals and your life-style."

Advanced color analysis offers a client-centered consultation in which expanded personal color palettes are selected that harmonize with both your essential qualities and your intentions. This means that color choices in our personal fashion design can reflect "who we are" and "what we want." Learning to incorporate color analysis and choices into personal fashion styling offers a valuable tool for expressing your personal appearance, essential values and present intentions. This includes your internal values, thoughts and emotions.

Today's palette is handmade of fashion fabrics with design and texture. A beautifully coordinated design scheme is presented to build an entire wardrobe that lends itself to mixing, matching and creating outfits with ease. You can have a smaller, more efficient wardrobe with incredible options for design. Closets are less crowded and you gain more quality clothing. Use these colors for everything—from eyeglasses to jewelry to makeup.

According to Evana Maggiore, author of *Fashion Feng Shui,* published in 2007 by Mansion Publishing Ltd, "Clothing is your body's most intimate environment and, therefore, energetically influences your life in the same way that your home and business decors do."

You can incorporate color on three different levels: essence, intention and personal color theory.

Essence is honoring who you truly are. It refers to your core traits and value system—your real nature and what you are in your heart. It is about being congruent with your values and presenting your authentic self.

Intention is all about where you are going, what you want more of and what you want to bring into your life. It is a resolve to act in a certain way or attract something into your life in the direction toward which you are moving.

Personal color theory is about your appearance; what people "see" on the outside. It embraces your eye, skin, hair and blush coloring. What we behold is what we enhance and work with.

> *"Mere color can speak to the soul in a thousand different ways."*
> —Oscar Wilde, Irish author, poet, playwright

Dress to Express With Color

Each color has its own wavelength and frequency and produces different emotional, physical and mental effects. You can use color to boost energy or create calm, to make people take notice or make them smile. Think about the day you have planned, your intentions and the effect you want to have on others. Choose a color that will help you communicate that message and set your intention.

Intensities of color communicate different levels of power and energy and reflect your intention:

- **Shaded colors are touched with black.** They are the darkest colors—black, charcoal, midnight blue and other dark tones. Wear these colors when your intention is to bring more wisdom, artistry and sensitivity into your life. Your motto for shaded colors: *creativity, serenity, calm.*

- **Tinted colors are touched with white.** They are fresh and clear tones. Wear these colors when your intention is to bring more expansion, motivation and learning into your life. Your motto for tinted colors: *vigor, action, growth.*

- **Saturated colors are the closest thing to pure pigment.** They are both psychologically "warm" colors and bright colors. Wear these colors when your intention is to bring more enthusiasm, connection and warmth into your life. Your motto for saturated colors: *life, love, laughter.*

- **Toasted colors are touched with siennas or umbers.** They are browns, taupes, tans and beiges. Wear these earth tones when your intention is to bring more tradition, commitment and support into your life. Your motto for toasted colors: *loyalty, security, stability.*

- **Muted colors are touched with grey.** They are soft colors, all shades of grey and lighter neutrals. Wear muted colors when your intention is to bring more organization, completion and refinement into your life. Your motto for muted colors: *beauty, order, quality.*

Here are three of my clients and how we used color for intention.

Jesse has such a wonderful personality. The moment you meet him, you fall in total like with him. Always having things to say, things to do and places to be, he is alive and fun. He was a conscientious traveling emergency room nurse, saving lives every day. Now he is a conscientious recovery room nurse who assists patients who are just coming out of anesthesia. His hours are long, emotional and demanding. Still, Jesse modeled, given his glorious good looks with dark brown wavy hair, green/hazel eyes and tan skin.

Jesse was exhausted, stressed and worn out; his life needed to change. He stated, "I am feeling somewhat empty in regards to my dress. I embrace style and want more sophistication with a refined look." He has excellent taste and after wearing hospital scrubs, he would just put on very casual clothing. After working together, we added more quality, luxurious fabrics in his life. Using muted hues in a monochromatic style brings richness to his dressing. Jesse can now dress with a redefined purpose. His intent is to attract status—and with these colors, he will.

Jennifer has an engaging personality. The moment you meet her, you are in awe of her. She simply exudes congeniality and kindness. Her job as a Regional Sales Executive is a position of great responsibility, as she is the "face of the company." Her position requires her to frequently host social events for her clients. Her days are long, detail-filled and busy. Jennifer turns heads with her striking good looks. She has deep brunette hair with subtle blonde highlights, beige skin and piercing blue-grey eyes.

Jennifer was close to exhaustion, burnt out and needing a change. As we talked, she said she wanted "to simply BE and have a sense of Zen, natural energy and complete peace of mind at work and at home." Her intent is to attract more serenity in her life, and with shaded hues, she will. She can now dress with a redefined purpose. We looked at deep grays and midnight blues, as these colors are stunning on her, and added flowing fabrics to her wardrobe.

Nancy has a glorious personality. The moment you meet her, you see a unique blending of sweetness, caring and fun. She places a high priority on her private practice as a therapist. In addition, she provides group therapy and has recently added weekend seminars. Her work requires careful attention to her wardrobe as she expands and grows. Nancy is a classic beauty with very striking brown hair, deep brown eyes and ivory skin.

Nancy stated, "As I look back on all the 'life lessons' I have learned, I now am ready to share my information as well as my experiences to help others." As we searched for her intention, we narrowed it down to "expansion." A long-time fan of designer clothing, Nancy needed to look the part of someone rolling up their sleeves and going to work to get things done. Tinted hues of blue and green were a nice addition to help Nancy attract more action in her life.

This is why I work as a personal consultant/personal designer—for the joy and life changes I see clients create in their lives; the "knowing themselves just a little better" which changes their lives forever.

Reveal Your Inner Beauty

Use color to reveal your inner beauty, express and resonate with your intention and enhance your own personal image color. Wear it for the impact it has on you and the people around you, and how it makes you feel when you wear it.

A certified professional color consultant can help you blend considerations of appearance, personality and intentions in ways that reflect and inspire your persona, dreams, potential and desires.

*"One's self-image is the most important belief
in one's belief system. It's the primary definer of what I can do
and the primary limiter of what I undertake.
Self-image directs me to be who I am, what I am,
and how well I perform. Change my self-image and not only do I
change, but the whole world changes—for the better."*
—author unknown

Think of yourself as a blank canvas and clothing as wearable art. Start each day with a goal of adorning yourself in your most alluring, becoming, exciting colors. What woman does not want to feel joy each morning when she opens her closet and dresses for the day in a palette of colors that are truly about her and her life!

CYNTHIA LEE MILLER, AICI FLC
The Art of Dressing & Style

Your first expression of who you are to those you meet

(913) 339-8764
cynthia@cynthialeemiller.com
www.cynthialeemiller.com

Cynthia champions the individual and assists in self-discovery and the outward manifestation of inner beauty. She helps her clients create a signature style that is both self-expressive and empowering, and leaves her clients with a redefined confidence in who they are and how they project their image to the world. Cynthia's vibrancy, effervescence, giving and energetic spirit and infectious enthusiasm serve her well in creating beauty with passion and purpose.

Trained and certified by well-known industry leaders, Cynthia has a passion for fashion that spans more than 22 years. She has expertise in the clothing industry, image consulting and color analysis. Her desire to work more closely and in-depth with her clientele was the inspiration behind her specialty studio. Advanced color analysis, custom body charting, Fashion Feng Shui®, custom clothing and jewelry, and vacation and trip packing are some of the services Cynthia offers.

Motivated and motivating, Cynthia is a professional speaker on the art of dressing and style. She is a member of the Association of Image Consultants International, International Image Institute, Association of Women Entrepreneurs, Fashion Societé and the International Feng Shui Guild – KC Metro Chapter.

Strut Your *Style*
Don't Just Believe in Miracles—Move Like One

By Chris Fulkerson

As a little girl, I watched the Miss America contest on television, captivated, as the contestants floated across the stage and gracefully descended the stairs, all the while exuding a grace and charm similar to the entrance Cinderella made when she entered the ball.

Projecting a positive self-image through proper posture, walking and movement isn't just for beauty queens or fairytale princesses. Taking care of yourself and your body begins with proper posture and movement. It affects your health, your mood and your business. Would you rather purchase something from someone standing erect or someone looking down at the ground? No matter what your job, you cannot inspire others if your shoulders are hunched or you're peering at your shoes.

People do not realize they have poor posture until they get a glimpse of themselves passing a mirror or window. Some need to be told. Maybe you have watched a video of yourself or seen your poor posture in a photograph. Whether you think you do or do not have proper posture, it is always a good idea to periodically check.

People view your healthy body as a sign of internal discipline and self-respect. When you respect yourself, it sends a signal that you likely respect others. Proper posture, movement and poise are the foundation of a healthy body. In a challenging economy, it is especially important to put your best foot forward—no pun intended.

Fundamentals of Good Posture

You know what poor posture looks like, whether it is a military stance or slouching. Need inspiration to maintain your posture? Post the following list where you can refer to it every day.

Why have good posture?

- Good posture supports your health and the proper functioning of internal organs.
- Poor posture puts stress on your spine and affects your nervous system, which controls your muscles.
- Good posture commands attention, gets results and earns respect.
- It makes you look ten pounds thinner.
- It creates the illusion of a larger chest by naturally lifting the ribcage.
- It enhances your image by sending positive signals through positive body language.
- Good posture helps you avoid back and neck pain.
- It allows you to breathe easier. Breathing is critical. According to my friend Kim Carpenter, DC, for every five degrees you bend forward, you lose a large capacity to breathe. Not getting the proper amount of oxygen flowing through your body accelerates the aging process.
- Good posture makes clothing hang and look better.

- It makes you look taller and more confident.

- It does away with negative thinking that can lower your self-esteem. Even if you don't feel like standing tall, fake it until you make it. Once you maintain good posture, you will begin to feel better.

- It increases your attractiveness through radiating self-assurance.

- Good posture communicates a positive message: 90 percent of all communication is through body language and how you carry yourself.

Good posture is the correct alignment of body parts supported by the right amount of muscle tension. You do not have to be erect and stiff to be taken seriously; however, no stance is more aging or negative than a hunched back and slouched shoulders.

Creating Proper Posture

It is one thing to *learn* proper posture and another to *maintain* proper posture. Old habits are hard to break. You need to establish a cue to trigger your memory to check your posture periodically. The telephone is a good trigger. Each time it rings, check your posture. Maybe you have chimes on a clock that ring on the hour to trigger you. Each time you pass a mirror, check your posture. Decide on your trigger and use it regularly to remind yourself to check your posture. Follow these steps to condition yourself to go beyond thinking about proper posture to maintaining proper posture.

- **Head.** Your head should sit on your shoulders. It is not designed to lead the rest of your body, nor follow it. Think of a string pulling up out of the top of your head. Allow the string to pull you up and lengthen your neckline.

- **Chin.** Your chin should be parallel to the ground. It is not designed to rest on your chest or to lift your nose in the air.

- **Shoulders.** The shoulders should be back and down. To achieve this, raise your shoulders to your earlobes, push the shoulders back then drop them down. Think: up, back and down. The palms of your hands should not rest against the front of your thighs but at the side of the thighs.

- **Ribcage.** Lift your ribcage out of your stomach but don't allow the ribs to pop out. The chest needs to be lifted and open.

- **Abs.** Many posture corrections can be made using your abdominals. The abs control your core; if your core is activated your entire posture changes. Activating your core is as simple as trying to pull your bellybutton back to your spine. Many years ago, I worked with a personal trainer who noticed I did not activate my core. She suggested I wear a girdle to remind me to pull in my stomach. The girdle was my trigger to remind me to pull my bellybutton back. Give it a try.

- **Buttocks.** Tuck your bottom slightly beneath your hips.

- **Knees.** Don't lock them. Keep a slight bend. This helps you walk with proper posture.

- **Feet.** Put equal weight on each foot.

With just a few adjustments, you can alter your entire look. Practice proper posture in front of a full-length mirror. Consistency is the key. Once you master your posture, be prepared for compliments.

Strut Your Style

Do you have the "it" factor—the ability to get a roomful of people to notice you at first glance? The stride of a confident person says, "I'm charismatic, friendly, interested and interesting." What does your walk say about you? What do you portray to the outside world with your walk? If you want to walk with more confidence, poise and style, practice the following steps.

Proper Walking Posture

- **Head.** Think tall. Keep your chin parallel to the ground. Don't look down, look forward. You can lower your eyes without dropping your chin.

- **Shoulders.** Remember—up, back, and down. Produce your arm movement from the shoulder, not the elbow.

- **Arms.** Maintain a natural swing. Allow your elbows to bend naturally to 90 degrees once your speed increases. Keep your elbows relaxed as your arms swing in opposition with your legs. Keep your arms close to your sides and avoid windshield wiper arms that swing across the front of your body.

- **Hands.** Hold them in a loose, closed-fist position in line with your forearm. Relaxed hands portray a relaxed individual. Squeezing them tightly indicates stress and does not allow healthy circulation through your fingers.

- **Chest.** Keep it lifted so it can expand fully and does not compress your internal organs.

- **Abs.** Keep them contracted to maintain good support for your lower back. Push your bellybutton to your spine.

- **Buttocks.** Tuck them slightly beneath your hips for better control. Squeeze the buttocks muscles to keep your legs engaged.

- **Hips.** As you walk, your hips naturally rotate as one goes forward and the other rotates back. As your speed increases, so does this rotation. Allow, rather than restrict, this rotation.

- **Legs.** Maintain a comfortable stride. Your knees will almost fully extend as you plant each foot onto the ground. Avoid locking your knees.

- **Feet.** Plant your heel first and then roll off your foot from heel to toe. Your back leg will push you forward. Moving that back leg forward faster increases your stride.

When you practice walking, choose the correct shoe and no more than a two-inch heel if you are not used to heels. Put your personality into your walk. Videotape yourself walking to decide what you want to change. Be calm, avoid rushing and show your confidence, not only by your walk, but by your smile and cheerful demeanor.

Spatial Awareness

Many times in a business setting, you will notice the woman sitting in a boardroom with her papers and belongings compressed to one small area in front of her while the men at the table spread out. In group pictures, females often offer to crouch down in the front so everyone can get in the picture. It does not serve you to be small and crouched. Inspire others by being fully aware of your surroundings. Stand out, catch attention and be polished with graceful mannerisms.

Each behavior change will change other behaviors. Using your physical space frees you to allow more space between your arms and torso. You cannot be graceful when trying to keep body parts closed in. Command space and be at ease while doing it.

Hands

Women often struggle with what they should do with their hands. Playing with your hair or fidgeting shows nervousness. Keep your hands off your face and never put your fingers near or in your mouth unless you are resting your chin on the knuckles of one hand. It also shows weakness to push your hands into your pockets unless you leave out the thumb or other fingers. When sitting, hands can be on your lap with both palms facing down or the bottom hand palm up and the top hand palm down. Don't overuse your hands in conversations. When in a social setting, keep your drink in your left hand so your right hand remains dry for shaking hands.

Fingers are sensual. We can learn from ballerinas' hands. When they dance, their thumb and middle finger connect. When picking up something, be aware of the space between your arm and your torso and grasp the object with the thumb and middle finger leading. Try this when reaching for a glass. Make sure your elbow, not your shoulder, drives the movement. Notice the difference when you approach the glass with spatial awareness and dancer's fingers. This gives you the "it" factor.

Making an Entrance
Walking into a room full of people can feel intimidating, especially when all eyes are on you. If you need to close the door when you enter, pull or push it closed behind you while entering to avoid turning your back to everyone.

Sitting
Approach a chair from the side. Feel the back of your chair with your leg so you do not have to look behind you. Bend the knees and use your thigh muscles to lower yourself to the edge of the chair. Knees should be together and shifted to the right or left. Then slide back into the chair. While sitting, you can cross your feet at the ankles with your feet remaining behind the knees. This is known as the royal family pose. If you want to cross your legs, cross the leg in the direction you are sitting. For example, if the knees are rotated to the right, cross your right over left. If the knees are rotated to the left, cross left over right. The legs should lie flat on each other. If you cannot do this, it is best not to cross your legs because you will be tempted to swing the top leg as you sit.

When rising from a chair, uncross your legs or ankles and place your feet flat on the floor. Use your arms to push yourself to the edge of the chair. Maintaining perfect posture, use your thigh muscles to stand straight up. The upper body should never hoist you up.

Descending Stairs

Walking down stairs can become an Olympic event, depending on the stairs, your heel height and your hem length. If there is a handrail, angle your body toward the rail to descend at an angle. Use the handrail for balance, even if you think you don't need it. The thigh muscles should do the work, keeping the knees slightly bent with each step. This will keep you from clunking down the stairs. You can look down without actually dropping your chin. Extra caution needs to be used when wearing pants with cuffs. Watch that your heel does not step into the cuff and trip you. When wearing a long dress, use your free hand to slightly lift up the dress.

In and Out of Cars

Nothing is more embarrassing than trying to get in or out of a car in a tight skirt or dress. It can be done with grace and poise. Approach the car as you do a chair. Back up to the seat, being careful not to brush dirt on your clothing. Lower yourself using the thigh muscles. Keeping your knees together, lift the legs and feet together and rotate your body into the car. Exiting the car, use your arms for balance, keep your legs and feet together and rotate your body. Using your arms, push yourself to the edge of the seat and rise using your thigh muscles.

Picking Up Objects

If not done correctly, bending over to pick up an object can not only embarrass you, but it can injure your lower back. Approach the object from the side. If wearing a skirt, smooth the skirt under your legs so the heel of your shoe does not catch in the hem. Bend from the thigh muscles and lower your body, maintaining perfect posture. Have the object in your hand before you rise. If the object is heavy, be sure it is in both hands before rising, so you do not lose your balance.

Poise

Poise comes with an understanding and experience of free movement. Balance is vital for poise and can improve with yoga or Pilates. However, just changing your balance and posture does not give you poise. Poise is good posture through movement and a positive attitude. Poise is the embodiment of your thoughts, feelings and beliefs. Poise is a fluid, dynamic way of expressing yourself through your attitude.

Attitude Has Everything to Do With It

Your state of mind influences your movement. Have you heard the saying, "You are what you think?" Attitude determines beauty and beauty starts on the inside with how you think. You cannot think bad thoughts and walk with your head held high. It is no accident that many phrases used to describe how one looks relate to posture and walking: "She has a spring in her step," "He's walking tall," "Her head's held high." People sometimes refer to others as being "balanced" and "centered," words used to describe posture as well.

Life is about making choices and you choose your attitude on a daily basis, negative or positive. Chemist George Washington Carver said that 99 percent of all failures come from people who have a habit of making excuses. No excuses! Quit lowering your head, slumping or looking sulky. Smile and enjoy your new, confident posture and walk. Walk tall and strut your style.

CHRIS FULKERSON

VIP Studio – Visual Impact and Presence

Where confidence that is seen on the outside is felt on the inside

(502) 939-6000

chris@vipstudioonline.com

www.vipstudioonline.com

*C*hris has been in the image business all her life. Voted by *The Voice-Tribune* (August 2006) in the top five Best Dressed in Louisville, Kentucky, she is an image and fashion icon in her community. For more than 25 years, Chris has inspired females of all ages, teaching modeling, image and fashion classes. Representing the Jana Kos Collection, Chris has worked with countless clients on closet audits, built complete wardrobes for high-profile individuals and produced and presented fashion shows for retail stores, associations, charitable organizations and the Kentucky Derby Festival fashion show.

After becoming internationally trained as a certified image consultant through the London Image Institute, Chris founded VIP Studio in Louisville. She is a member of Fashion Group International and the Association of Image Consultants International.

Besides writing articles and being a frequent radio and television guest, Chris was commissioned as an image consultant for the book, *How to Look Stylish* by Annette Welsford. She is currently writing her own book, due out in 2010.

Shapes *of* Style
Dressing for Your Body Shape

By Lisa Ann Martin

Every woman has a beautiful, yet unique and manageable body. Learning to live with and love your body, instead of fighting the challenges, is essential to looking and feeling great.

Have unsuccessful shopping trips led you to believe nothing out in the marketplace was made for your body and that nothing will ever fit correctly and look good, no matter what the style, fit or shape of the clothes? If so, you are like many women who suffer from insecurity and frustration about their bodies and see only their flaws.

The reality is this: You can change the silhouette of your body, look slimmer, create or show off curves, elongate your body, play up your assets and move the focus away from trouble areas by wearing correctly fitting clothes.

The goal of correctly dressing for your body type is to enhance your assets—while dealing with challenging areas of your body—to help create the best possible look. When you select the correct clothes to show off what you love about you and camouflage what you dislike, you begin to feel more confident with your clothing and your body.

Identify Your Body Shape

The starting point to developing your own personal style is correctly identifying your body shape. Most stylish women do not have perfect bodies, but they have learned what to wear and what to avoid. They choose clothing that accentuates their assets and minimizes their less-than-perfect areas.

Once you determine your shape, you can begin to purchase clothing that has the correct cut and fit. The fears and anxieties you have about your body will start to fade when you look great in the silhouettes that flatter and enhance your assets.

There are four different universal body types: Diamond, Hourglass, Pear and Rectangle.

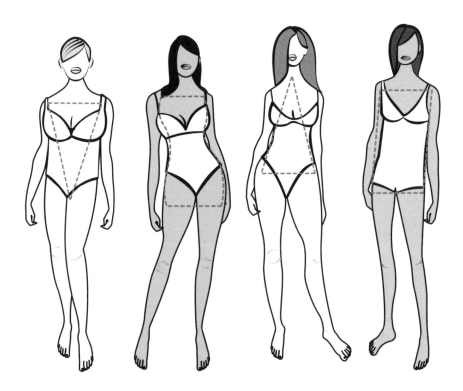

Diamond Shape: Your shoulders and/or bust are larger than your hips.

Hourglass Shape: Your shoulders and hips are about the same size and you have a very defined waist.

Pear Shape: Your hips are wider than your shoulders.

Rectangle Shape: Your shoulders, bust and hips are similar in size and your waistline is undefined. A variation on this shape is the Oval, where the waist is slightly larger than the other measurements.

By taking four simple measurements, you can determine the basic shape closest to your own body shape and use it as a guide to define and develop your own personal style. Start by taking some measurements.

- Shoulders: Measure your shoulders from the edge of one shoulder to the edge of the other shoulder.

- Bust: Place a tape measure under the arms and run it around the fullest part of the bust and across the shoulder blades.

- Waist: Run the tape measure flat around the natural waistline, just above the belly button. Allow one finger space between the tape and body for a comfortable fit.

- Hips: Stand with feet together and run a tape measure around the fullest part of the hips below the hipbone.

Now that you have your measurements, you can choose garments that enhance your body in all the right ways based on your body type.

> *"A woman's dress should be like a barbed-wire fence:*
> *serving its purpose without obstructing the view."*
> —Sophia Loren, Italian actress

Diamond Shape

The diamond-shaped body generally has broad shoulders, a large bust and upper back, a narrowing at the waist and hips, and slender legs. If you have a Diamond shape, the blessings are plentiful: great cleavage, slim torso and knockout legs. The main concern with this shape is top-heaviness. Dress to draw attention to the bottom half of your body and create an illusion of balance by accentuating your smaller hips and legs.

Choose the following for a figure-flattering silhouette:

- Darker colors on top and lighter colors on the bottom to balance your overall figure and minimize the top half
- Shirts with a straight look and little or no detail
- V-necks and wrap tops that draw attention away from wide shoulders
- Tunics and flared or fitted tops that offer a soft, skimming definition and pull the eye to the center of the body
- Larger-strapped tank tops with a deep neck or V-neck that balance the lower body
- Wide-legged, flared or boot-cut pants that balance out the larger upper half of the body
- Skirts and dresses with a bit of shape and wide hemlines such as A-line, softly pleated or tulip hemlines that draw attention to your shapely legs
- Jackets that flare at the waist and add volume

Avoid:

- Tube tops, tops with thin straps or puffed sleeves, strapless tops, turtlenecks and crewnecks, since they draw attention to your wide shoulders
- Skinny jeans or leggings that accentuate slim legs
- Tight or pencil skirts that accent top-heaviness
- Shoulder pads

"The dress is a vase which the body follows.
My clothes are like modules in which bodies move."
—Pierre Cardin, French fashion designer

Hourglass Shape

The hourglass-shaped body generally has shoulders and hips that are similar in size and a defined waistline. The benefits of this shape are a balanced, curvy body and a small waist. Your goal is to embrace the curves and maintain a balanced silhouette.

Wear the following to enhance your appearance and give a figure flattering silhouette:

- Wrap, fitted-shift and belted shirtdresses that follow the lines of your body
- V-neck and scoop-neck fitted tops that reveal a hint of cleavage and draw the eye up to your chest
- Fitted shirts that hug your curves
- Jackets with a nipped-in waist and a curved lapel
- Trench-style, belted coats
- A-line, wrap and pencil skirts with the hem at or just above your knee to show off your legs
- Mid-rise pants, such as boot-cut or slightly flared styles, that minimize your hips and balance your body
- Soft fabrics that drape and skim the body

Avoid:

- Fabrics that add bulk to your body and hide your curves
- Empire dresses and loose-fitting dresses that disguise your defined waist
- Crop tops and loose, baggy peasant tops that hide the body

- Boxy, double-breasted and oversized jackets that hide your body's shape

- Bell-shaped, boxy and pleated skirts that add volume to your hips

- Low-rise jeans that make you look heavier

Pear Shape

The pear-shaped body generally has hips and thighs that are wider than the shoulders or bust. This shape has several exciting features—sexy hips, a shapely bottom and a slim waistline. The goal is to widen your shoulder line, place the focus on the upper body and minimize the lower body in order to visually restore balance.

Try the following to achieve a figure-flattering silhouette:

- Dark colors on the bottom that add a slimming effect

- Bright or lighter colors with texture and patterns on top to broaden the shoulders, bust and upper torso

- Fabrics such as light knits and matte jersey that accentuate and smooth out the curves

- Necklines such as boat, scoop and V-necks that create a broader shoulder and reveal a narrow mid-section

- Shirts with small shoulder pads or breast pockets that add volume

- Pants with little or no waistband that flare slightly or have ease through the legs, and straight-leg or boot-cut jeans; wear at the natural waist or a little lower

- Skirts that drape over the hips, such A-line, wrap or fit and flare; wear just below the knee

- Empire, strapless, wraps and off-the-shoulder dresses that help balance the body shape

- Monochromatic mix-and-match separates that help create a balanced, elongated look

- Accessories that draw the eye upward

Avoid:

- Pleats, side pockets and details on backside pockets
- Circle, bias-cut and pleated skirts that add unnecessary volume to your hips
- Drop-waist or tunic styles that hide the waistline and cover the backside
- Pants with narrow or tapered legs

> *"The dress must follow the body of a woman, not the body following the shape of the dress."*
> —Hubert de Givenchy, French fashion designer

Rectangle Shape

The rectangle-shaped body generally has shoulders, bust, waist and hips that are all equal in size. You have a "boyish" style figure since your body is straight up and down. Your best features are your arms and legs, and your main concern is defining your waist. This goal can be achieved by widening the shoulders and adding curves to the hips to provide the illusion of an hourglass silhouette.

Here are several ways to achieve a figure-flattering silhouette:

- Shoulder pads, tops with V-necks and U-necks, and wrap tops that flatter and create a curvy figure
- Tops with details around the hip and corset tops that give your body shape
- Boot-cut jeans with a dropped waistline that adds some curves
- Belted jackets like a trench that help create an hourglass silhouette
- Jackets with structure or that cinch at the waistline to add curves

- Belted, empire or wrap dresses that create a defined waist
- A-line, flared, circle and wrapped skirts that have waistlines and taper outward to create curves
- Accessories that draw the eye upward

Avoid:

- Loose garments that add to the rectangle shape
- Patterns with vertical lines
- Wide or straight-legged pants that accentuate your boxy shape
- Clingy fabrics that emphasize your boxy figure
- Square-necked dresses that accent the straight lines of the boxy body shape
- Pencil skirts without a waistband, especially ankle-length skirts
- Long, straight-cut and double-breasted coats that square off the body shape

"Fashions fade, but style is eternal."
—Yves Saint-Laurent, French fashion designer

Style Begins with the Proper Foundations

Undergarments are everything—the basis of every great look. A properly fitting bra, panty and/or body shaper will make a world of difference in the way you dress and in the way your clothing fits and flatters your body. Every outfit starts with the foundation pieces.

Your daily choice of undergarments should not only be dictated by your body shape, but also by the type of outfit you plan to wear. Your undergarments need to fit properly and complement the shape of your clothes. By wearing properly fitting undergarments, you can visually drop pounds in an instant.

Bras and panties should fit snugly without binding, riding up or creating unsightly bulges. To remain in total control of your body shape and make it appear sleek and bulge-free, you may consider body shapers, which come in a wide range of support and styles like the all-in-one or tummy-control. Worn in the correct size, it will offer extra support while remaining comfortable to wear.

As far as color is concerned, you always want to match your undergarments with your outfit, especially if wearing white clothing. Choosing a skin-tone undergarment is always a safe choice.

For more about shapewear, see Sandy Moore's chapter, *It's Not Your Grandma's Girdle,* on page 117.

Ten Wardrobe Essentials to Fit Your Body Shape

When it comes to building a functional wardrobe, first assess your lifestyle. No matter the particular situation, whether it is casual or professional, there are ten pieces you need in your wardrobe to look sharp and well dressed. These closet essentials are the backbone of every stylish woman's wardrobe. They may be worn almost year-round and do not follow any particular fashion trends. With these basic garments in place, you will be ready to dress for any situation and feel totally prepared.

When you choose your top ten, make sure to follow the guidelines for your body shape using the tips in this chapter. For example, if you have a rectangular shape, choose a little black dress with a defined waist.

1. Little black dress
2. Classic white shirt
3. Dark denim jeans
4. Cashmere cardigan sweater

5. Pencil or A-line skirt

6. Dress pants in a neutral color—black, grey or khaki

7. Blazer

8. Trench coat

9. Classic suit with pants and/or matching skirt

10. Accessories—Ballet flats, high heels, a great purse for day and one for night, a classic watch and sunglasses

Wardrobe Rescues

Now that you know what to wear and what to shop for, what do you do with your current wardrobe? Here are some tips for turning not-so-flattering garments into more flattering ones without having to replace your entire wardrobe. Go through your closet and accessories and make these quick rescues to your existing wardrobe.

Rescue for Diamond Shapes:

Draw the eye away from your upper body.

• Pair dark colored tops with lighter colored bottoms.

• Nip in your waist with a belt, but wear it slightly below your natural waistline.

• Remove shoulder pads that add dimension to your shoulders.

Rescue for Hourglass Shapes:

• Cinch in your waist to accent your natural curves.

• Belt in garments that hang straight from the shoulder to show off your waist.

• Shorten tops so they just meet the top of your hips.

• Use a large scarf like a sarong. Drape it diagonally across your lower half to create a soft feminine look.

Rescue for Pear Shapes:

- Pair light-colored tops with darker-colored bottoms.
- Wear several necklaces together to draw the eye upward.
- Shorten jackets and tops to end at the hips.

Rescue for Rectangle Shapes:

- Add shoulder pads to jackets and tops.
- Add belts to straight-up-and-down garments to accent your waist.
- Take tucks in loose-fitting tops to pull in the waist

Dressing for your body shape is a matter of understanding proportions and knowing how to focus the eye on your body's assets and away from its challenging areas. Pay attention to your body shape and the tips for choosing garments that serve that shape. Make sure your clothing is the right size for you and invest in well-fitting undergarments, especially bras and body shapers.

Wearing figure-flattering clothing can enhance your image and create a pleasing silhouette. Always purchase the highest quality possible, since quality pieces will fit best and retain their value. Think of your wardrobe as an important investment that you cannot afford to pass on. It is always good to be the best-dressed woman in the room.

> *"Feel free to play with trends—but always be faithful to your personality and lifestyle."*
> —Randolph Duke, American fashion designer

Take some time to discover what your best assets are, as well as your challenging areas. This way, you will learn what to accentuate and flaunt, as well as what imperfections to minimize. We all have assets, and we all have challenging areas, and it is only a matter of accentuating the positive and camouflaging the negative.

LISA ANN MARTIN
Lisa Shops & Stealth Styling

(480) 773–2677
lisa@lisashops.com
www.lisashops.com
www.stealthstyling.com

*L*isa Ann Martin, an image stylist and versatile entrepreneur, enables people to coordinate their inner and outer beauty. She empowers clients to promote a confident personal brand image that fuels success, providing a holistic styling approach.

Lisa Ann is a recognized expert in the field of both men's and women's image consulting and basic dating etiquette. Her many accomplishments include exclusive columns in *Perfectify Magazine, Phoenix Men's Guide Magazine* and *Women on Course.* She has been featured in regional, national and Canadian publications, along with frequent radio and television guest spots. Her blogs, "Fashionably Minded" and "Essential Guy" are a great source of fashion, image and dating advice. She is currently a member of Fashion Group International, as well as the Association of Image Consultants International, and is involved with several local Arizona charitable organizations.

Lisa Ann worked many years in the financial and corporate charity arenas, and recently produced a satellite radio show. This array of experiences, dealing with a variety of personas, continuing to learn about the importance of appearance and the impression it can leave upon a person within seconds, all led to the pursuit of her passion: style.

Stepping Out of Sweatpants And *Into* Style

Look Your Personal Best *Every* Day—*No Excuses!*

By Debbie Wright

"The badly dressed woman, people remember the clothes. With a well-dressed woman, they remember the woman."
—Coco Chanel, French fashion designer

*W*hat does your daily personal presentation say about you? I have spent over two decades with beautiful women learning that many women feel that it doesn't matter how they look. I have found in particular, that women who have a casual lifestyle feel that their current, day-to-day schedules do not warrant looking their best. I am here to tell you that, regardless of your size, lifestyle or budget, you deserve to present your best self each and every day of your life. Your image, your confidence and your self–awareness should be celebrated each day. Each daily decision you make matters and has its effect. What we eat, what we learn, what we teach, how we treat others and how we present ourselves—it all matters.

You make first impressions every day whether you are at the grocery store, at a playgroup, working or lunching with friends. When you respect yourself, others will respect you in return. Learning how to dress beautifully and appropriately for your body *today,* will directly affect your emotions, your confidence and your accomplishments on a daily basis. My dream is for every woman to feel beautiful and confident at every wonderful stage of her life.

Throughout your life, you continue to grow and learn from your experiences. Your image and style should also evolve and grow with you. You deserve to improve with age. Your knowledge and experience, combined with a desire to be better, will enhance your life in all areas. When you feel good about yourself, you are a better daughter, wife, friend, girlfriend and mother.

Your positive energy envelops you and will positively affect those around you, too. The most common question I am asked is how to continue feeling confident either after children or during menopause. There is no doubt that as women, our bodies go through tremendous changes throughout our lives. The reality is that gravity can also work against us as we age. I have five tips to share that will help you begin to regain positive energy and confidence with your style and personal presentation. I refer to them as my fashion high-fives.

Fashion High–Fives

1. Dress for who you are *today* and how you look *today.* Live in the Now. How can you begin seeing yourself as a beautiful woman if you don't begin seeing and acknowledging your individual beauty? The personal beauty that only you can own and believe begins inside you. Stepping out of your current "dress down" attitude begins with recognizing that at every stage of our life, although we may not be at our perfect weight or size, we have features we need to accentuate and others we need to minimize. Regardless of body type, you need to choose clothing that helps to create an hourglass shape. This is the quintessential body proportion. Everything is in balance. Your choices in clothing can actually create balance in the body you have and you can have the body you want!

2. Accentuate your best body feature with clothing. You wear 20 percent of your clothing 80 percent of the time. Make certain that your 20 percent consists of clothing that makes you feel confident and flatters your figure. For example, most women either carry extra weight around the middle or in the thighs or legs. If you carry the weight in your middle, select clothing that draws attention to your great legs. Choose jeans that are dark in color and have a straight leg for a great casual basic. The average woman wears jeans four times per week, so your jeans should flatter your figure and boost your confidence. Buy jeans that offer some stretch. I suggest buying one size down in stretch jeans. This will ensure that the fit is perfect when they're worn and stretched. You deserve to feel great in your jeans and by doing so, you hop on the confidence train and good habits begin to take shape!

"Fashion is architecture; it is a matter of proportions."
—Coco Chanel, French fashion designer

If you have a small waist, choose clothing that accentuates this feature while keeping your pants darker in color to balance your frame. Boot-cut pant styles provide balance, and a dark wash is a clean look that offers versatility. Dark jeans can be dressed down with a cute tee and fun accessory for a more casual, daytime look or dressed up with a great jacket for evening. Look for waist-enhancing details in your fitted tops. Seaming or gathering details that highlight the waist are perfect styles for you. Wearing a belt around the waist can also provide a nice silhouette. Also, be sure you choose styles that define the shoulders. Blouses, T-shirts and tops that have seaming in the shoulders are often the better, body-complimenting choice.

3. Get a new, quality, properly-fitting bra every season. Chances are, you are one of the 80 percent of women who is wearing the wrong size bra. Wearing the correct size bra absolutely affects how your clothes fit. Get your bra measurements taken by a professional and invest in a couple of good bras. I recommend one in nude and one in black. Whether you are small or big busted, proper support will help to elongate your torso and you will look better in your clothing. It is also healthy for your body to ensure that you are wearing the correct bra size. Get measured a few times per year, as our bodies continue to shift and change as we age. While it is usually okay to machine-wash your bras, you shouldn't dry them in the dryer. Your bras will last longer if they are washed and left to air dry.

I recently conducted my own fashion poll and asked women to meet me at the local mall to see if they were in fact wearing the wrong size bra. All ten of the women who came to be measured were wearing the wrong size bra. The most shocking discovery was that eight of the ten were off by two whole sizes. You can imagine the significant change the right size bras made in how these women looked in their clothing. They felt more pulled together and more attractive. Treat yourself to a proper bra fitting; you will be amazed at the results. Each and every client I work with goes for a bra fitting before we begin our style journey together. It sets the foundation for the clothing and the precedent for having great fit and style.

4. Stay polished and always wear flattering accessories. Polish and accessories are the icing on the cake of your personal style. Whether you are wearing a casual white T-shirt and jeans or going out for the evening, accessories pull an outfit together and add great style. Fashionable scarves that come in all shapes and sizes can add wonderful color to a basic tee and can take an outfit from boring to beautiful. Have fun wearing layered pearls with a white tee and jeans. Or choose interesting earrings that stand out if you want to keep your neckline clean. Chunky bracelets and big rings also add a fun element and a little zing. When selecting accessories, choose items that make you smile. Look through fashion magazines and see what you admire most about the accessories being shown. Notice how they are being worn. If you doubt your own sense of style, look at current fashion magazines, see what you are drawn to and duplicate it. You can find many similar styles and looks in local stores. Consignment stores offer a fun variety of accessories that are unique, special and often one-of-a-kind.

> *"A girl should be two things: classy and fabulous."*
> —Coco Chanel, French fashion designer

Accessories offer a way to express your individuality. Get an instant update each season by adding a fun new purse to your wardrobe or a stylish new coat. These are items that frame your figure and enhance your style. One of the most popular services I offer clients is a "wardrobe reinvention." I take jackets and tops that they already own and turn them into new outfits. I re-invent the item by using accessories and showing the client how to layer and accent. This takes an "ordinary" item and makes it extraordinary. It is an easy way to update your wardrobe without spending a lot of money. You will be thrilled when you begin to see how many options you can have with a single piece by simply changing how you wear it. For example, let's talk about the basic white T-shirt. You can make a simple, classic and elegant statement by choosing a multi-strand of pearls to accent the tee worn with jeans. You can choose a more bold and colorful necklace to create a fun look. You might also layer the tee under a denim jacket (or any jacket) and add multiple brooches to the jacket. Scarves can also spice up a basic tee. However, if you layer your T-shirt under a fitted, colorful print jacket, you might opt to wear great earrings. You don't want to compete with the print of the jacket with a necklace or scarf. The accessory should add the punch without being overpowering. For more on how accessories can enhance your personal style, read *Accessory Challenge! Meet Your New BFF,* by Dominique Vaughan-Russell on page 105.

Because staying polished is so important, you never want to lose perspective of its impact on how you feel each and every day. Make certain your nails look clean and manicured and that your hair—whether pulled back or blown dry—looks good. These are the little things that can make all the difference in how you start your day. They begin the flow of energy in the right direction. Taking care of yourself doesn't necessarily require an abundance of time.

If your hair is something that you struggle with day to day, consult your hairdresser for some simple options. I am a great example of this dilemma. I have very coarse hair and in my busy life I recognized that I did not dedicate the time I needed to for my hair to look its best. I asked the expert, my hair stylist, for advice. I now go in for a blow-out twice a week with my hairdresser and my hair has never looked better. He and I worked out the price so it wouldn't be too costly for me to see him weekly. This has alleviated a lot of stress for me and I now feel more confident about how my hair looks. There are always options to explore! The lesson to be learned is that you can look as good as you desire to look. It's easy and affordable. You deserve to be treated like a superstar and to look like a superstar, every day.

5. You can shop *anywhere.* You don't have to spend a lot of money to have great style. Once you begin the self-acceptance of living in the now, you will begin appreciating your best body features. You will recognize that you are uniquely beautiful and that no one else can claim *your* personal beauty presentation. You own it.

You can now shop anywhere—once you have assessed your current lifestyle and wardrobe needs. With this done, you can shop anywhere from large discount department stores to high-end boutiques, from thrift stores to online outlets.

Here are your casual wardrobe staples, the building blocks for all lifestyle needs. Think of these items as the foundation to create multiple wardrobe looks:

- **At least one nude and one black bra.** These are wardrobe essentials that build the foundation for all outfits.

- **Two pairs of dark denim jeans that you feel great in.** One pair should be hemmed to accommodate flat shoes for a more casual look, and the other should be hemmed for the heel that you are most comfortable wearing, for a dressier look.

- **Tops and jackets that help to create an hourglass shape.** They have features that create a curve without being tight.

- **Basic white and black T-shirts.** These are staple pieces that should be replaced each season. They offer the versatility to be worn alone with great accessories or layered under jackets and sweaters.

- **White cotton blouse.** This timeless classic works well dressed down with jeans, layered under jackets or worn under a suit. Choose one that has a special detail like French cuffs or a unique collar.

- **Black fitted jacket.** Fashion and function. A black jacket is a wonderful investment to make regardless of your current lifestyle. Worn casually or worn over a dress or as a suiting separate, this is a great item to own. Watch the fit, make sure it flatters.

- **The Little Black Dress.** The must-have basic in every woman's closet. Choose a style that celebrates your personality. Look for a dress silhouette that enhances your waist and showcases your best features. Keep an open neckline if you are petite.

- **Accessories.** Necklaces, scarves (colors that enhance your eyes are best when framing your face), bracelets, rings and brooches.

Be Your Best Today—Embrace Your Body Blessings

Clothing can absolutely enhance your body shape and create confidence in how you present yourself. The beauty of having great style and taking pride in yourself daily is having the "inner attractiveness" to match. Our inner and outer beauty equation will and must complement one another. Our outward confidence and energy shines most brilliantly when it is paired with truth. Be honest, live pure and accept yourself for who you are.

Be the best you can be—every day. You deserve it!

DEBBIE WRIGHT
Project Closet

I create more than outfits,
I create confident women.

(860) 331-7094
debbie@projectcloset.com
www.projectcloset.com

*D*ebbie Wright was born and raised in Connecticut and has been a professional wardrobe consultant since 1991. Seen every Tuesday on *Better CT TV,* Channel 3, WFSB, Debbie is most noted for her ambush makeover segment, fashion news and trend reporting. She can also be heard weekly on CBS Radio, *The Damon Scott Show,* reporting her style finds and giving fashion advice to commuters on their drive home. Her background in wardrobing began at Ann Taylor stores where she managed and opened new stores in Connecticut and Massachusetts. Through her extensive retail and corporate experience working for top Fortune 100 companies, she now has a portfolio of clients that spans the country. Project Closet opened its doors in 1997, offering personal shopping services, closet makeovers, image workshops and fashion show production.

Keeping on top of trends and knowing how to interpret them to meet her clients' needs, lifestyle and budget continues to be one of Debbie's proudest attributes. She can help ANYONE develop great personal style and confidence that translates into empowering people to live the life they deserve—one of complete abundance in health, money and relationships.

Accessory *Challenge!*
Meet Your New BFF

By Dominique Vaughan-Russell, AICI FLC

I challenge you! Rejuvenate your wardrobe. Create new and exciting uses for your accessories. Get the most out of your BFF (Best Friend Forever).

The Challenge: I invite you to stretch your imagination. First, delve deep into your closets, rummage through the bottoms of those drawers and come up with a pile of long-lost, little-used accessories. Now you can add some more recently-purchased accessories to create an entirely new wardrobe inventory. To help you with the process, just imagine you are a finalist on a reality fashion game show called "Change It Up!" Go wild and have some fun with this.

The Rules: Here are your parameters for this fun challenge. You will be given only two basic outfits:

1. Dark-wash straight-leg jeans with a basic white T-shirt

2. A little black dress (LBD) with a matching jacket

Now you are faced with a week jam-packed with work and social events.

Your Goal: To come up with the most diverse, innovative and attractive outfits possible, using just accessories added to your two basics above.

Remember, the look must be appropriate to a myriad of activities and venues. Your only limitation on putting together the perfect outfit is your imagination.

The Rewards: I wish I could wave my magic wand and reward the "winner" with a lifetime supply of Manolo Blahnik shoes! But if you accept this challenge there are some very tangible payoffs.

You will:

• Know what accessories you currently own and are overlooking, and can now organize and interchange them.

• Have a much better idea of what your "must-have, multitasking, go-anywhere-do-anything" accessory items are.

• Discover what missing essentials you need to add to your existing wardrobe inventory.

• Realize you are much more creative than you ever thought possible!

Accessories Really *Are* a Girl's Best Friend

Who doesn't want to save money? By finding different ways of using the same accessory, using that accessory on a different outfit, or buying a few new accessories each season to update your basic wardrobe, you will save a bundle. This is by far the easiest and most cost-effective way of updating or reinventing any outfit. Plus, you can change the mood and feel of your outfit to reflect your mood or the occasion.

As an added bonus, accessories are absolutely your best friends on any trip. They enable you to pack just a few basics but still come up with any number of dynamite looks to fit any business or social obligation.

Let's get started. Using the selection of clothes from the challenge, I will use myself as the person I am dressing for these situations. You, of course, will dress according to your own body type, age and personality. Read through the examples, and then it will be your turn to "survive" a challenging week with just the basics.

The Art of Creating Many Looks with Very Little Effort

The Jean. Start with a basic straight-leg jean in a dark wash (splurge on a pair that fits you perfectly), and a basic good quality white or off-white T-shirt. This is an outfit that will take you from the beach to a club or nice restaurant—from shopping with your friend in your neighborhood boutiques to walking the Champs-Élysées in Paris. Let us explore ways to make this work; not forgetting you can use the jacket from the LBD to enhance the look or for warmth.

- **The beach.** I will roll up my jeans just above the ankle; wear nice colorful sandals and a printed scarf tied around my waist as a belt, and carry a funky canvas beach bag. Top it off with large, fun sunglasses, hoop earrings, and a sunhat. Voila, beach ready!

- **An upscale restaurant.** Here I trade my sandals for nice high-heeled shoes in a neutral tone (or boots, depending on the season), a designer belt in a neutral color, lots of silver necklaces, my favorite rings, a silver cuff bracelet and small earrings. My purse is a medium-sized, neutral-toned shoulder bag. For a splash of color, a dramatic neck scarf.

- **A fun club.** Since I only have the white T-shirt to work with, I will add some funky jewelry and some sparkle around my waist. My highest and funkiest platform shoes are called for here, with a wide silver belt low on my hips. I add a big, chunky rhinestone bracelet and a coordinating ring and earrings, a long, thin knit scarf wound once around my neck with the ends hanging down, and a glittery comb or band in my hair. My small purse would be silver or black and shoulder-slung for safety.

- **Shopping with a friend at local boutiques.** Comfortable ballet slippers, or flat boots to save my feet the agony of heels from all that walking. A belt with a distinguishing buckle, a colorful scarf wrapped twice around my neck, a fun but sophisticated silver bracelet and earrings and a large leather sack purse would complete the outfit.

- **Ah, and now for my trip to Paris.** I would be understatedly elegant —much the same as if I were shopping in the designer district in my home city. However, I would up the sophistication level by wearing my diamond rings and earrings and tying an Hermès scarf around a designer purse strap, or tying it loosely around my neck. I will tie back my hair in a low ponytail with a tortoise shell barrette, and my color choices for the whole ensemble are neutral and elegant.

See how easy and fun that was?

The LBD (Little Black Dress). Now imagine yourself in all those same situations, but with just your little black dress plus jacket for style or cool weather. Many of the same accessories work to create the same feel, but you can exchange a few of them to make the outfit work better, or shuffle it all up and invent a completely new look.

- **The beach.** As with the jeans, I could choose to wear nice colorful sandals, a printed scarf around my waist as a belt, and a funky canvas beach bag. Large fun sunglasses, hoop earrings, and a sunhat. That would all work with the LBD, but here's another look. A thin black belt around my waist to hitch up the skirt into a shorter length, metallic sandals, a large black sunhat with the scarf tied around the brim, large black sunglasses à la Jackie O, a collection of multicolored wide plastic bangles on my wrist and the funky canvas beach bag. Now I have created a more sophisticated and elegant look. Both are perfectly acceptable and completely different.

- **An upscale restaurant.** My classic pumps or high-heeled boots remain, but I am adding sheer stockings. Lose the belt, but still keep my many silver necklaces, favorite rings and bracelet. The medium-sized, neutral-toned shoulder bag will also stay the same, but I will exchange the scarf for a pashmina in a favorite color. In this instance there was little change except for removing the belt and changing the scarf—so simple, yet what a difference.

- **A fun club.** Going to a club is always a challenge for me. There is that fine line between too much glamour and looking dowdy and totally out of place. The LBD is a great staple to own as it is so versatile, but what to do with the basic dress to make it more "hip." I am going to put on opaque tights, either some platform-soled knee-length boots, or some fun black ankle boots. Next, a wide black belt around my hips to make it look a little more figure-hugging and exchange the rhinestone ring and earrings for some long mod necklaces. No shiny scarf, and the shoulder slung purse is the wrong look here; I will take the little metallic clutch.

- **Shopping with a friend at the local boutiques.** Remember I chose comfortable ballet slippers, or flat boots for comfort when I was in my jeans? With my LBD, I will stay with the flat or low-heeled shoes, and possibly the boots, but will add a pair of fun, colorful opaque tights which will take the outfit from bland and boring to a more fashion-forward, stylish look. I will forego the belt but keep the colorful scarf wrapped around my neck, picking up the same colors as are in my tights. My fun silver bracelet and earrings and a large leather sack purse also stay with me as they are my favorites and I am most comfortable wearing them.

- **Off to Paris.** My LBD makes elegance easy, but I will be wearing my very best pumps and sheer stockings, my diamond rings and earrings, a designer scarf, loosely tied in front around my neck or around the shoulder strap of my stylish designer purse. The tortoise shell barrette is a classy accessory and an easy way to pull back my hair and create a more refined look, so I will keep that too.

Express Yourself

As you can see, I have changed very little on each outfit, but have been able to create ten very distinct looks. By taking one casual set of clothing and one little sophisticated dress, you can make them individual, unique and appropriate with the innovative use of accessories.

- Remember, these accessories were all selected based on my personality, body type and age. When you do your accessorizing for the challenge below, keep your own personal brand in mind. All your accessories should be an extension and expression of your personality.

- For example, dramatic and bold accessories, such as bright, shiny, angular pieces in black or red would look completely out of place on a small, curly-haired, freckled redhead with a romantic personality. She should be wearing delicate antique jewelry and ruffles. When browsing the season's fashion trends, do not follow blindly; be true to yourself and make the looks reflect you.

- Take trends and make them your own through accessories. A color that is hot this season but not in your color palette can be an accent color in a scarf. If big and chunky jewelry is in, but you have very fine bone structure, modify the scale of the pieces accordingly.

- If miniskirts are in and your legs are not your finest feature, shorten your skirts a little, but wear opaque tights and bring the focus up around your face with brighter colors or an eye-catching accessory.

Now It's Your Turn

You already know the wardrobe rules—jeans, T-shirt and LBD, so here's your ultimate challenge: A week full of very different events and activities to make the most of your accessory artistry.

Itinerary for Your One-Week Challenge:

Office Monday through Friday—including casual Friday

Monday night—daughter's or son's soccer game

Thursday night—Dinner with the president of the company at the city's best restaurant

Friday night—Birthday party for a best friend at a trendy nightclub

Saturday afternoon—Shopping with a girlfriend in the high-end designer stores

Saturday night—Date with your significant other at a smart, casual restaurant

Sunday noon—Company picnic with the office staff

Sunday night—Backyard barbecue with good friends

The Challenge:

- Use all your own accessories
- No two outfits can be repeated
- Mix and match any combination of clothes from the allotted selection only (jeans, white T-shirt, LBD and jacket)

Monday Day: Work
Night: Daughter's or son's soccer game
Tuesday Day: Work, board meeting
Night: Dinner at home

Wednesday Day: Work
Night: Dinner at home
Thursday Day: Work
Night: Dinner with the company president at the best restaurant in town
Friday Day: Work, casual Friday
Night: Birthday party for a 30-year-old good friend at a trendy nightclub
Saturday Day: Shopping with a girlfriend in high-end designer stores
Night: Date with your significant other at a smart casual restaurant
Sunday Day: Company picnic with the office staff
Night: Backyard barbecue with your good friends

What Is Missing?

What did you discover? Any accessories you could have used in many instances but were missing in your accessory inventory? Any pieces you may be overusing because you have not thought of alternatives before now? Here are a few BFFs that no woman should be without.

The Three Things People Notice First

We all aim to make a good first impression, so make sure these invaluable staples are in excellent condition and the best quality you can afford.

• A killer pair of heels; dress them up or down with jeans, a dress or a suit

• One really good purse—do not economize here and never, ever buy a knockoff

• A good quality watch, the best you can afford

Other Indispensables

• A pashmina. Every woman should have a collection of pashminas in a variety of colors; they will take you anywhere, anyplace as a cover up, an accent, a winter scarf, or just for warmth

• A large, everyday purse

• A neutral, evening purse

• A pair of metallic sandals

• Designer sunglasses

• One good belt that fits through pant loops or may be worn on its own

Trendy Seasonal Purchases to Update Your Wardrobe on a Budget

• Shells (sleeveless tops) in this season's colors

• Fun shoes in this season's new heel style

• A scarf in the hot new color

• A piece of costume jewelry that suits your personality and updates your look

Who hasn't wished for a magic wand? Isn't every girl's dream to be able to wish for something and have it magically appear? Let your dreams come true, for just a while . . . imagine the possibilities. Wave your magic wand, use your imagination, and shine like a star.

Now you are all set to change things up, rejuvenate and reinvent your wardrobe. Come up with as many varied, new and exciting combinations as you want. Be creative, and above all, have fun.

Remember, accessories are a girl's Best Friend Forever!

DOMINIQUE VAUGHAN-RUSSELL, AICI FLC

Vaughan-Russell Image Consulting

You only have five seconds to make a first impression

(416) 804-7898

dominique@vaughanrussell.com

www.vaughanrussell.com

*D*ominique Vaughan-Russell is an expert in image enhancement and personal branding. Specializing in color, body and personality assessments, Dominique maximizes wardrobe, grooming and etiquette potential for both men and women. Yet, Dominique goes far beyond the superficial concept of "personal makeovers." She understands the important role confidence and presence play in achieving both career and personal goals and objectives.

Dominique's extensive career in the fashion and design business encompasses more than 25 years of experience in the image consultancy business. As a global traveler, she is able to spot hot international trends and incorporate their influence on clients' appearance as well as being well-versed in international cultures and customs.

Dominique is a dynamic international presenter and guest speaker. Her confident style and sophisticated elegance inspire clients to realize their full potential. She is a graduate of the International Image Institute and has a degree in Fashion Merchandising, in addition to certificates in Professional Modeling and Makeup. Dominique is a member of AICI, the Association of Image Consultants International.

It's *Not* Your Grandma's Girdle
Discover Today's Shapewear—
A Hot New Take on an Old Tradition

By Sandy Moore, AICI CIP

"Wearing a corset certainly changes your state of mind."
—Radha Mitchell, Australian actress

In case you haven't noticed, a shapewear revolution is sweeping the country. Around for thousands of years, shapewear has suddenly become the hot new item of the day and has moved from the back of our collective lingerie drawer to its new place of honor, front and center. This is a revolution you don't want to miss out on.

Why Shapewear, Why Now?

By 2008, baby boomers, people between the age of 44 and 62, were the largest portion of the workforce (41.5 percent). And what are boomers obsessed with? Looking and staying young and fit. Though 50 may be the new 40 or even the new 30, nature and gravity will still have their way. Regardless of how young in spirit you are, your body will eventually give you away. One delightfully simple strategy for recapturing a more youthful silhouette and renewed sense of vigor is to slip into one of today's shapewear creations. Instantly, the years melt away. Your bum is lifted, the girls are perkier and your tummy is flatter.

What could be better! Baby boomers, while not alone in their interest in shapewear, are certainly driving the trend.

The renewed interest in shapewear may also reflect a healthy rejection of the recent trend toward slovenliness. For some time, we have all been subjected to a seemingly endless stream of muffin tops, back fat and belly rolls. Everywhere you look, at the mall, the grocery store or driving down the street, you are visually assaulted by unruly mounds of flesh spilling over and out. When did it become okay to, literally, let it all hang out? Judging by the growing shapewear industry sales statistics, fewer and fewer women are comfortable being quite so relaxed!

It helps that today's shapewear is, in every way, not your grandma's girdle. In fact, most manufacturers don't even use the term girdle today, preferring instead terms like panty shaper or body reshaper. If, when you hear the word shapewear, you immediately think of that less-than-friendly garment you wore in high school, then it is definitely time for you to discover what your daughters already know. Today, it is possible to look sleek, trim and curvy without giving up the comfort you have grown to expect.

And don't think shapewear is only for the plus-size woman or the over 40 crowd. Compression shapewear is very popular among young women who want a little extra smoothing out. Young and trim does not necessarily mean fit, and as a friend who lives in New York said, "Thin is never thin enough." Shapewear can be any woman's secret for looking great in her clothes. With more women than ever wearing shapewear and more choices than ever to consider, it's a great time to take another look at your options.

Are You Red Carpet Ready?

If you have ever looked in wonder and amazement at the Hollywood glitterati on Oscar or Emmy night, understand that beneath all the finery, there is very likely more than a perfectly toned body. Wardrobe stylists work closely with the stars and know what is underneath.

"Roughly 80 percent of the women and 50 percent of the men walking the red carpet are wearing shapewear. I've never had an actor (male or female) be offended when I suggested they wear shapewear. Actors are all about their public image and anything that can enhance or improve that is more than welcome."
—Kami Gray, American TV/film wardrobe stylist and author

Notice I am not talking about women only. While the number of women wearing shapewear clearly exceeds the number of men, shapewear is an equal opportunity resource.

"I did a movie with Duke Wayne and was very surprised to find out he had small feet, wore lifts, and a corset. Hollywood is seldom what it seems."
–Rock Hudson, American film star

We are all influenced by the hip and glossy style that originates in Hollywood and is popularized in the media. The truth is, we all have red carpet moments in our lives; times when we want to dazzle and to create an illusion of perfection. Take a tip from the stylists and let shapewear work its magic.

Shapewear Isn't New

Over the centuries, men, women and even children as young as seven or eight years old have regularly worn garments for the sole purpose of coaxing their bodies into the socially desirable silhouette of the day.

The history of shapewear reflects the history of fashion, the ever-changing ideals of beauty and the social attitudes of the day.

Shapewear has always had a lot to do with women's breasts, at some times glorifying and at others diminishing their importance. Some of the earliest known examples date back roughly 4000 years to the ancient Minoans who lived on what is today the Greek island of Crete. This was a time when a woman wore her corset on the outside rather than underneath her clothes. If you thought Madonna started the trend, think again. Not only did the Minoans beat her to it, they also outdid her. Minoan corsets cinched in the waist, raised the breasts and left them fully exposed for all to see. What today would be considered pornographic, seemed natural in a culture that worshiped female divinities.

Now you see them, now you don't. During the Middle Ages, the spread of Christianity and the idea of original sin redefined attitudes about the human body. The body became something to be distrusted, rather than glorified, and this attitude was reflected in the shapewear of the day. By the 1300s, French high society was wearing a form of corset designed to straighten and tame the figure. Still worn over a woman's outwear, the goal now was to minimize a woman's curves, especially her breasts. The word corset itself derives from the French word *cors,* a diminutive meaning body.

By the 1500s, corsets were widespread throughout Europe. Since then, styles have evolved and changed to reflect the fashion of the day, but one thing remained constant. With few exceptions—a brief period following the French revolution, the heyday of the flat-chested 1920s and the feminist bra burning 1960s—shapewear has continued in vogue.

120

A Shapewear Revolution

So if shapewear has been around for thousands of years, what sets the shapewear of today apart from those earlier versions? Well, quite a lot.

Shapewear was originally fashioned using generally unsympathetic materials. When women first stepped into something like a corset, probably during the Bronze Age, the garments were made of Bronze Age materials. Wood, bronze, and stiff animal hide were likely the materials of choice and you can bet comfort was not top of mind. Later, corsets relied on cane, whalebone, iron, stiff canvas and paste to provide the requisite rigidity. It is not surprising that by the 1870s, corsets were seen as having a disciplinary function as well as a fashion role. By holding the body in a constrained and upright position the corset was believed to encourage restrained and upright social behavior.

Luckily for us, everything began to change in 1939, when polyamide (nylon), the first commercial synthetic fabric, hit the scene. Suddenly, there was this new material that was both lightweight and strong. In 1959, another giant leap forward occurred with the introduction of elastane (spandex or Lycra®). As the name suggests, it has extra-ordinary elasticity. It can stretch up to 500 percent, and has a recovery rate of 95 percent. Shapewear designers began to combine polyamide and elastane, modern shapewear was born and its slow and steady rise in popularity began.

Comfort is the mantra of our day. Of course you want to look good, but are you willing to give up comfort in the process? Most women want to have it all and why shouldn't they? But when forced to make a choice, comfort almost always wins out. Luckily, you no longer have to choose. Compression garments made of elastane and polyamide have largely replaced more traditional corsetry. They deliver figure-flattering results and they do it with maximum comfort.

If, however, you are after the ultimate va-va-va-voom experience, then a corset or corset-inspired garment is still your best choice. Even today's corsets deliver a brand new level of comfort due to the new materials and fabrications now available.

Health and Fitness Benefits

Increased awareness around issues of health and fitness is another factor driving the shapewear revolution. Manufacturers advertise that shapewear can improve your posture, help you lose pounds and inches, drop dress sizes, improve your general health and wellness and even boost your athletic performance. While some of these claims may be inflated, it's also clear that shapewear can have positive health benefits.

Orthopedic specialists have collaborated on many new shapewear designs with the express goal of creating garments that provide increased back support. If you have ever put on a corset, a panty reshaper designed for lumbar support or even a well-designed compression garment, you know that your back immediately feels more supported. Some shapewear garments, for example, the BodyMagic and Men's Abdomen Shirt by Ardyss International, are recognized by the insurance industry as reimbursable when prescribed by your doctor. If you suffer from back pain, experiment with various shapewear options. Back pain relief may be only a shapewear garment away.

Is your posture less than perfect? I'm sure you heard it from your mother, "Stand up straight." As it turns out, she was giving you very good advice. Posture is closely related to health and fitness. In fact, it is virtually impossible to experience maximum mental clarity and physical vigor if you have poor posture.

> *"... faulty posture is not only the leading cause of back pain,*
> *it also . . . reduces the flow of blood and oxygen to the brain, it*
> *decreases mental alertness, undermines one's ability to concentrate*
> *and even contributes to an attitude of cynicism and gloominess."*
> –Susan Bixler and Lisa Scherrer Dugan,
> American leadership development experts, authors

Given this sobering information, it is good to know that many of today's shapewear designs can radically improve your posture. A corset or similarly structured garment improves posture by incorporating elements of vertical rigidity into their construction. If corsetry is not your thing, the next best choice is a medium- to high-compression garment made from quality power mesh fabric. It provides much the same benefit with none of the restriction. Look for an upper-body shaper that has an 'X' pattern built into the structure of the back. These garments exert a gentle backward pressure on the shoulders, helping to open and raise the chest, allowing room for the lungs to expand and work at maximum efficiency. Discover just how great you feel when you are standing up straight!

Look Younger and Thinner Instantly!

As years pass, muscle tone is lost and posture suffers. Additionally, women must often deal with the effects of osteoporosis, which weakens bones. The result is a stooped silhouette in which the distance between the bustline and waistline is reduced. This creates a very matronly stance. As soon as the girls start pointing at the floor, you are certain to be offered the senior discount when go to pay the check. I'm all for a discount, but if you are not ready to flash your AARP card just yet, shapewear can save the day!

As you add years and life experience, you are also likely to add pounds. I know it's not fair. A few of you will even manage to avoid those dreaded extra pounds, but for most of us, the ticking of the clock, childbirth and menopause eventually result in an increase in and a redistribution of weight. You will start to look in the mirror and wonder where you went and where this slightly chunky evil twin came from.

Not to worry. You will not have to look hard to find body-cinching shapewear that can actually take you down in inches and dress sizes. You can recapture your former waistline. "How much can I lose," you ask? The answer, "More than you imagined." Ardyss International is one manufacturer that advertises an instant reduction of two to three dress sizes. You will, of course, give up something in comfort if you want to achieve such dramatic results, but seeing yourself so utterly transformed can make it all worthwhile, especially if there is a red carpet event in the near future.

I used to be all about comfort. Then I tried on a body shaper designed for maximum effect, looked in the mirror and saw Jayne Mansfield staring back at me. I couldn't stop staring at myself. Now I sometimes opt for that more structured garment just because I like the way it makes me feel. Yes, I still value comfort, but having a handsome man standing next to you at Starbucks raise his eyebrows slightly and tell you look great provides a comfort all its own.

Reclaiming Sassy

When you are 30, 40, 50, 60 or older, it can be a challenge to look in the mirror and like what you see. As the decades pass, things start going south. Your bum, your breasts, everything really, starts shifting as gravity has its way. What was up is, if not down, at least headed in that direction. So what's a girl to do? If you are not ready to become invisible, and I hope you aren't, you are probably already looking for ways to inject new life and vigor into your style. Today's new shapewear is an affordable, effective and noninvasive strategy for reclaiming your sassy former self.

Say Yes to the Shapewear!

For over 4000 years women have been saying yes to shapewear. It has been how women have redefined their silhouettes, boosted their confidence and expressed their personal styles and fashion sense. But never before have there been so many options and never before has shapewear been so comfortable to wear.

Today, there is a shapewear option for every body and every figure challenge. There are corsets that will give you an hourglass figure to rival the most voluptuous Hollywood hottie and there are lightweight compression garments that will oh-so-gently smooth out offending bumps and bulges. Whether you want to achieve dramatic results or subtle changes, there is a product that is right for you.

So what are you waiting for? There has never been a better time to stock your lingerie drawer with shapewear. Try on styles you have never worn before. Step out of your comfort zone and be adventurous. As a reward, you will be ready for your next red carpet moment. Just as important, you will be ready to look and feel your personal best every day of the week.

SANDY MOORE, AICI CIP
Image Talks, LLC

Reshape your image, reshape your life

(503) 256-1497
sandy@imagetalks.com
www.imagetalks.com

*S*andy was nurtured by three extraordinary women who helped shape her unique style as an image consultant and trainer. Her loving mother Alicia, who cleaned house with a feather duster, wearing heels, a stylish dress and pearls, taught her the importance of always looking your best. Her irrepressible Aunt Fontelle, who at age 14 was six feet tall and towered over all her peers, taught her the power of standing tall in the world. And her talented grandmother Theodosia, who taught her that looking exceptional does not depend on your budget. Whether working one-on-one with clients or delivering a corporate seminar, Sandy brings can-do energy and a sensitive approach to her work.

Passionate about making image education more affordable, Sandy launched the first online training course focused on developing the soft skills necessary for professional success. Colleges and nonprofits in Canada and the United States have adopted her online curriculum.

In 2005, Sandy earned recognition from the Association of Image Consultants International as a Certified Image Professional, one of the premier certifications available to image consultants and trainers. She previously served on AICI's International Board as VP of Member Communications.

Work **Your Wardrobe**
How to Turn Heads and Get Noticed

By Carrie Leum

The difference between getting dressed and getting noticed is like the difference between the personal styles of Dolly Parton and the Dalai Lama. While much of what we are discussing in this book applies to all aspects of your life, here I will focus on adding inspired style to your work life. In the working world, you can turn heads, create more awareness of your contribution and create a brand for yourself by adding a dash of spice to your look.

Think about it: when it comes to selling an idea or inspiring others, visuals are paramount. That's why each year, millions are spent on Super Bowl commercials and selecting designer gowns for the red carpet. Compelling visuals are the reason that YouTube has become a phenomenon. Thanks to the bright colors and graphics, you likely did judge this book by its cover, and that's okay.

As a personal stylist and president of Corset Personal Styling, a national wardrobing service, my days are spent helping women define their look to stand out and get ahead in their careers. Whether I am speaking to women about wardrobing at a Fortune 500 company, dressing models for TV show fashion segments or conducting a personalized styling session, women want to know how to step outside their comfort zones and capture the attention of their superiors or potential clients.

Your personal appearance is about so much more than what you wear. It can actually serve as a visual cue of your work performance and your working personality. After all, you want your financial advisor to be rolling in cash, your aerobics instructor to be toned and muscular and your personal stylist to be on the cusp of every fashion trend. According to business owners and senior executives we have interviewed, a casual outfit may make people wonder if they can trust you with their money. Likewise, a disheveled look may make you appear disorganized, and a lackluster style may translate as lack of creativity. Is that the impression you are going for?

In a survey we conducted about the importance of personal appearance in the workplace, 25 percent of the business owners and executives admitted to withholding an employee's promotion due to issues with her personal appearance.

The key to standing out is to be memorable. For example, anyone can toss on a navy blue pantsuit, sensible black pumps and a white blouse and head out the door. There is nothing wrong with this outfit, except it lacks a sense of personality. There is no way to determine whether she is a flight attendant, a museum docent or a business consultant. To others, her look is generic.

Now, imagine her friend in the same basic outfit. Add a layered necklace, an interesting pair of earrings and a pair of pumps with a chic cheetah print. Immediately, you imagine a woman who is creative, smart and on top of her game. Now—and this is where things get interesting—imagine that you are hiring one of these women to consult on a special project that requires creative and strategic thinking. Which woman would you choose?

Following are some tips to help you make a statement that can translate into opportunities and paychecks:

The "How Tos" of Getting Noticed

Creating a look that will get you noticed does not need to be a chore. First, follow the rules of professional and appropriate wardrobing for the workplace. Be aware of your company's policies and dress code. Secondly, determine how you will use your look to make your mark and differentiate yourself from others in your field. In the tips that follow, I outline ways to jumpstart this effort.

Inject Personality, But Not Too Much

A young fashionista with an eclectic style, I entered the work force in the early 90s. I was confident with my look and rebelled against a conservative corporate style when I went to work for a major public relations firm in Chicago. Luckily for me, our vice president sat me down at review time and said that I could go far in my career if I adopted a more business-oriented look. So, despite an entry level salary, I marched into the nearest Casual Corner shop, invested in three suits from the clearance rack, and mixed and matched them until the cows came home. I never lost sight of who I was and found a way to let my true personality shine through by adding statement-making accessories, shoes and hair styles. Once I asked a client, whose company dressed casually in jeans and logo gear every day, if we should dress more casually for our meetings. She said, "Absolutely not, we love seeing what you wear—it helps us know what's in style and on trend."

Stand Out

Now in the fashion business, I can be little more rebellious again. When I turned 40, I wanted to keep my mojo and got a wide red strip added to my already-highlighted bangs. At first, I was unsure if it was necessary at my new age, but soon I was being recognized for this stand-out look. I found that it was actually helping me build my personal brand. I cannot tell you how many compliments I receive or people who ask me if I work in the fashion business. It's a great conversation-starter. I know this look is not for everyone or for every profession, but it is my way of making a statement.

Know Your Stature and Silhouette

There are also tricks to dress for your size. If you are smaller statured, patterns and texture can help you stand out. Layer your looks, such as a ruffled blouse under a vest, or use a wide belt to create added interest with a basic jacket and blouse. If you are a larger woman, be careful not to go over the top and keep your look sleek with bold statement pieces. A size 26 client told me that she is sick of finding clothing featuring clown appliqués or balloons. Agreed. There's a polished, on-trend look for everyone—you may just have to kiss a few toads and try on some dowdy dresses to find it.

Dress for the Job You Want

Once you know where you want to be in your career, you can begin to aspire to that role. Start dressing for that position, but be sure to inject your personality into the look.

Now that we have covered the basics, here are some initial strategies to jumpstart your personal styling efforts:

Closet Refresh

I am a fashion consultant for the Twin Cities' ABC affiliate and have conducted "Closet Takeover" segments in which I check out women's closets and help them get inspired by their existing wardrobe. During the segment, the women show me an outfit they typically wear, and then I select key pieces from their own closets that add more personality and pizzazz to the looks. Everyone should have a takeover of her closet! Once a year, have a friend come into your closet to help you look at your pieces in a new way. Someone else can see the love in an old sweater, or combine a new belt with a great skirt you haven't worn in years. I recently donned a pair of earrings from my high school prom for an event, practically guaranteeing that no one else had on the same thing.

Coming and Going

When we conduct Working Wardrobe seminars for women in corporate America, they want to know how to stand out, even though they are shopping at the same places. To avoid seeing your look "coming and going," be wary of shopping just one or two department store collections. Instead, select a jacket from one brand and then head elsewhere to find a coordinating blouse. Consider shopping at boutiques or consignment stores for interesting garments that will layer with and enhance your investment pieces. And do not forget that your accessories can be the biggest way for you to personalize a party look.

Add Spark and Sparkle

Many women have limited creativity when it comes to sparkle. Somehow over the years they have learned that sparkle and shimmer should be reserved for holiday parties. Ladies, there's nothing wrong with a little sparkle. In fact, blinged-out pieces with shiny or shimmery accents, such as crystal or cubic zirconia, reflect light onto your face. While we're not recommending that you wear a sequined gown to your next business meeting, an easy way to make these pieces work for you is to keep the rest of your look simple when you select a shiny necklace or a studded accent piece. A gemstone brooch looks sharp on a black blazer and we applaud the juxtaposition of a crystal necklace with a tee and jeans on the weekend.

Play with Texture

One standout strategy I love is the mixture of textures. Pair a crisp corporate blouse with a fuzzy sweater or a faux fur cardigan. Layer a ruffled blouse under a tailored, fitted vest. Wear a leather jacket with a cashmere crew neck. Gone are the days of the sweater twin set as the business-casual uniform; by combining textures, you showcase a garment's character and add to your own.

Color Wheel

No different from decorating your home, there are some colors that look terrific when combined, even without patterns bringing the colors together: pink and green; purple and red; and turquoise and brown. If you are confident with sampling color combinations, the sky's the limit in terms of creating looks that are uniquely you. Try using multi-color accessories to tie various solid-color garments together—it is a great way to extend the number of outfit options in your closet. Be careful not to mix colors that connote seasons or sports teams, such as red and green; orange and brown; or purple and yellow.

Pop It

Don't be afraid of adding color or texture. If you are like most women and boast a closet full of basic black, a bright necklace can be your new best friend. Learn to use "pop" colors in your dressing. A lemony bright yellow tee or a hot pink blouse make a terrific pop color under a black jacket. The combination is great with black trousers, denim or white pants. I just bought a pair of plaid trousers on sale. Black is a key color, but so are ivory, orange, and olive green. Because the pants are so busy, I could opt for a black top; or I can step the look up and pair the pants with an orange tee and olive green military-inspired jacket. Black boots ground the entire look and keep it from getting "costumey."

Tone on Tone

While we are fans of contrasting colors, I cannot say enough about the richness of a tone-on-tone look. We love a rich camel top and jacket over a pair of black pants. Or a vibrant red blouse and sweater wrap over a grey tweed skirt. Once you have this rich foundation, you can use accessories to amplify your outfit—a colorful scarf, interesting tights or a fun belt can complete the look.

Leather and Lace

Don't be afraid to introduce your girly clothes to an alter ego. We love a lace tee under a leather jacket, a studded belt with a classic fitted sweater, or a preppy cardigan with a wild print blouse.

Icing on the Cake

No one but you can determine your look—that's what makes clothes and accessories such critical tools in your briefcase. But there is more to accessorizing than wearing a necklace and earrings. It is the combinations you create that define your style and turn heads.

Whether you are a Jackie O classic pearls and sunglasses girl, or an anything-goes Cyndi Lauper lady, one way to get noticed is with interesting accessories that can help better define your personality. Explore these tips for getting accessories to work for you:

- Layer pieces for more impact—wear more than one strand and weight of pearls, beads or gold/silver necklaces.

- Don't be afraid to mix gold and silver or other metals; the result can be dramatic.

- Break out of "matchy-matchy" mode; mix and match your necklaces, earrings and bracelets.

- If you're like most women and boast a closet full of basic black, a bright necklace can be your new best friend.

If you are someone who already accessorizes, take that look to rock star levels:

- Dig into Grandma's vintage pieces to find unusual gems.

- Play with your pieces—an ornate clip earring can become a pin or a pendant with a few adjustments.

- Swap out a standard necklace chain for a satin ribbon for added shine and the ability to adjust the length.

- Explore possibilities with scarves—there are so many lengths and ways to tie scarves.

Refresh and Revive

In a recent survey our company conducted with an executive women's magazine, a vast majority of the women surveyed (98 percent) said they thought personal appearance has a major impact on career success, yet 60 percent said they felt like they had nothing to wear. Although women said they spent between three and six weeks per year shopping for and planning their work wardrobes, it's clear that they were not building a thoughtful closet. The women shared several common pitfalls: buying way too much black, finding age-appropriate looks and not dressing the body they have "right now."

Here are some tips we recommend to help women break free from these issues and tap refreshed looks each season:

- Discover non-jewelry accessories—items like a scarf, colorful tights or a belt can inspire your look and take it from drab to divine.

- Invest in a statement piece—this item can be a colorful jacket, vest or cardigan that can mix and match with your wardrobe and resuscitate your black garments.

- Tap a bold piece of jewelry—find a piece that has talk value; something that is colorful, artistic, or vintage can make a white blouse and pair of black trousers into an attention-grabbing look.

- Dress it up—wear your dresses and skirts; because corporate offices are so casual these days, you will get more compliments if you step out in something dressier.

- Blouse on—add a new blouse to your closet each season; a patterned piece can update an old suit, ruffles will add texture to your look and more feminine tops balance out a masculine vest; and a crisp blouse layered under virtually anything in your closet can help you create endless looks that are still polished.

Creating a Lasting Impression

If you're ready to reinvent yourself, create a "look book" of celebrity fashions and magazine ads that inspire you. Take this book with you when you shop to make it easier to find the look that best suits you. Or work with an image professional or personal stylist to help you achieve your signature style.

Finally, before you jump in, follow these rules to ensure you get noticed for the right reasons.

1. Be sure you feel confident in your look.

2. Ensure that you are emphasizing your face.

3. Make sure you are dressing for the silhouette that works best for you.

4. Walk the talk—own your look.

5. Be ready to accept compliments—how will you respond?

But most of all, be ready to turn your noticeable self into business and networking opportunities that can propel you ahead in your career. Here's to compliments and lasting impressions.

CARRIE LEUM
Corset Personal Styling

Because you never get a second chance to make a first impression

(952) 224-2495
cleum@corsetstyling.com
www.corsetstyling.com

"Look the part" is Carrie Leum's fashion philosophy. A believer in the powerful dynamic between a styled look and a woman's self-esteem, work success and ability to meet personal goals, Leum is president and founder of Corset Personal Styling, a national wardrobing services company. Corset, which designs and manufactures its own private label, helps women pull their looks together for a polished, head-turning personal style. Her company sends wardrobes to clients each season and offers wearing and pairing tips to help them build a thoughtful closet. The company also specializes in dressing women with hard-to-fit silhouettes and sizes.

A twenty-year public relations veteran, Leum has dressed CEOs, brand spokespeople and celebrities for appearances on Oprah, CNN and the Today Show. As an agency owner, Leum has helped countless brands—Kohler®, MillerCoors®, SC Johnson Wax®, and Kohl's®—stand out and tell their stories.

Leum, an on-air fashion consultant to KSTP-TV (ABC) in Minneapolis/St. Paul, is the recipient of the Innovative Business Award from the National Association of Women Business Owners and has been named "Best Stylist" by *Minnesota Monthly*. She holds a bachelor's degree from the University of Wisconsin.

Face *Fashion*
Making Every Day of Your Life Beautiful

By Barbara Layne, PhD

$\mathcal{A}$s owner of the Academy of Makeup & Fashion, I have interviewed countless prospective students in this fascinating field of fashion, beauty and media makeup artistry. I listen for their desires to help other women boost their self-image and confidence in themselves, through their talent as an image and makeup professional.

Confidence is the key ingredient that keeps us heading in the direction of our dreams. For women, our appearance has something to do with that. When you feel happy with your look, do you act differently? Confidence is also about choosing to believe in your own instincts and standing firm in that choice. My goal in this chapter is to give you cosmetic beauty information that can help you make sound personal choices.

Inspired style comes from within your spirit. You have put your look together through a process of personal analysis, which includes understanding your personality, your activities and your personal preferences. Other important aspects to consider would be your coloring, lifestyle and what your image needs to say for you to accomplish your goals in life.

Your self-analysis in all these style subjects also holds true in your inspired style of makeup. Your makeup look is a crucial accessory to your personal style. Your cosmetics and the style of application should balance and complement your outfit. The truth is that people will notice your face first. The worst makeup mistake is to wear no makeup at all—a naked face is not the natural finished look desired. However, beautiful makeup does start with natural and healthy skin.

Creating the Perfect Canvas

Your makeup should not hide your skin; it should enhance your natural beauty. It's the canvas on which a beautiful painting is created. In my professional world of high definition film makeup, entertainment celebrities are pressed to take better care of their skin. The days of heavy makeup are over!

In today's busy world, no woman wants her beauty regimen to dominate her life. Keep it simple. Learn your skin type and find a skin care line with a cleanser that can both start your day and dissolve the makeup at night; an alcohol-free astringent or toner to follow the cleanser; a light day moisturizer; and finally, a night cream to hold your natural skin moisture as the body rests and repairs itself. How soon should you expect results? Products that work will show an improvement right away. Finally, remember to stay out of the hot midday sun. Protect, protect, protect!

Your Makeup Style Personality

You hold in your hands a masterpiece for personal or professional image making! *Inspired Style* is a book that offers a delightful compendium of real-life appearance issues and practical information.

There are enlightening exercises that guide you from the inside out to clarify and define your personal style. After you have done the homework, let's apply the makeup to complement your educated fashion style.

Just as with fashion, we are never locked in to just one makeup look. How boring! You have learned to focus on your basic fashion personality, but you also have the flexibility to allow for various social requirements or your moods! Are you a Natural, Classic, Romantic, Dramatic or Creative? All, you say? I have always said that the way we wear our makeup will give the man in our life a clue as to what mood we are in that day. They appreciate that!

Natural Face Fashion. This is a young lady who enjoys comfort and no fuss in her wardrobe, hair and makeup.

Her makeup: *simple.* Mascara, a little eyeliner and lip gloss. This works at home or playing sports. If you are in business with the public and you are over 21, I suggest adding a light foundation, neutral colors of eye shadow with the mascara and eyeliner, and a harmonious lipstick color with the gloss.

Classic Face Fashion. Her wardrobe is full of basics with a tailored cut; timeless.

Her makeup: *defined.* Have a steady hand, because this face fashion should be as tailored as the clothes. Define a beautiful arched eyebrow. Add a matte, neutral eye shadow color with a little shimmer. Follow with eyeliner and mascara. Define your cheekbones softly and match your lipstick with lip liner.

Romantic Face Fashion. She loves anything girly! Loves color and lots of clothes. She also likes to be noticed by the opposite sex. Her paycheck goes to all things pretty!

Her makeup: *soft but colorful.* Well blended, no edges. She wears shimmer on her eyes and sheer dewy cheek blush. On her lips, soft color and lots of gloss. She loves her hair extensions and strip eyelashes. For business credibility, think Classic, but blend it! Add the shimmer later in the evening.

Dramatic Face Fashion. Makeup artists love this lady. She is into the latest trend and wants to wear it first among her women friends. She also likes to be noticed. She is confident and sparkles when she enters a room. Women love her. However, she could be intimidating to an insecure man.

Her makeup: *edgy and colorful.* It could be bold. She wants to stand out in a confident, but not bizarre, way. In a business environment, show your confidence but tone it down.

Creative Face Fashion. Hopefully she works in a creative field because this woman must express herself with her look. It is a spiritual thing! She is fun, colorful, inventive and usually talkative.

Her makeup: *creatively different.* She doesn't want a makeup artist, she wants to do it all herself. Depending on her creative work, if she works in sales, tone it down until evening.

As you scan through fashion magazines, you will see these various styles represented. Notice the well-balanced look when the makeup coordinates with the fashion personality.

Assembling the Tools of the Trade

A great sight-appropriate mirror. If you wear glasses (or should), a quick look in a stronger mirror will save embarrassment later.

Sponges. Use a latex sponge that allows foundation to absorb into the sponge.

Velour puff. To apply loose, translucent face powder.

Tweezers. For brow shaping.

Brushes. Invest in the best brushes you can afford. Natural hair gives the smoothest application for powder products. Use synthetic hair brushes for cream products.

- Concealer brush: for darkness under eyes or red spots
- Powder brush: for setting the foundation
- Blush brush: for cheekbone accents
- Fluff brush—medium: to apply neutral base shadow
- Fluff brush—small: for detailed eye shadow
- Blending brush—medium: for final blending of color
- Angle brush: to detail outer eye color, eyeliner, eyebrows
- Eyeliner brush: when you want a narrow-line accent at the lash line
- Lip brush: to fill in the lips with lipstick color

Keep your brushes clean. Never soak them, because you might loosen the hairs from the handle.

Art and Science of the Transformation

Face proportions. Artful makeup is about bringing out our best features and compensating for those we are less fond of. A basic understanding of your proportions will help to determine what enhancements or corrections to make. You do not have to have a perfect oval face to be beautiful, yet the correction principles are based on this face shape.

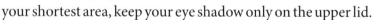
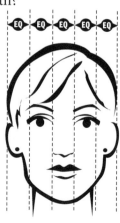

Is your face—vertically—in three equal parts?

- Longest from hairline to the eyebrows? Shade the hairline area subtly.

- Longest from eyebrow to under nose? Allows you space for beautiful smoky eyes. If this is your shortest area, keep your eye shadow only on the upper lid.

- Longest from nose to chin? You can shade the tip of your chin and jawline.

Is your face—horizontally—five eyes in width?

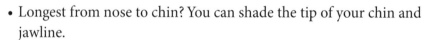

- If the width of one eye fits perfectly between your two eyes, then there is no particular eye shadow correction needed.

- If your eyes measure closer together, you have close-set eyes. Correct this by using a light-color eye shadow on the inner third of your eye. This creates the illusion of width.

- If your eyes measure wider than the width of one eye, you have wide-set eyes. Correct this by using a medium shade of eye shadow on the inner part of your eye. This creates the illusion of a more narrow area. Your eyebrows can also be tweezed slightly closer as well.

Watch your parallel lines for perfect eye shadow application. Look at the angle of your jaw, then the angle of just under your cheekbone. They are perfectly aligned!

The angle of your eye shadow application should have the same parallel alignment as the others. Your features will look balanced.

Makeup Made Simple

You don't need to be a makeup artist to look great. You have learned your best colors from other experts in the field, and you understand that these colors need to be in harmony with your skin tone. Therefore, you will not look overly made up. There is no need to buy closets full of clothes or drawers full of makeup when you understand your style principles. This understanding saves you time, money and frustration.

Here are some simple steps to selecting the right products and tips on how to quickly and artfully apply them for your most flattering look. Let's get started. Relax, experiment and have some fun!

Concealer

What it does: helps to disguise discolorations anywhere on the face.

Concealers come in light to heavy formulations. Choose according to the severity of your coloration challenge.

Under-eye darkness: The under-eye area is most challenging for many women. To correct the color, you want the concealer to be slightly lighter than your skin tone.

If the coloration is *blue:* an orange-base cream will neutralize the blue.

If the coloration is *brown:* use a pink-base cream to neutralize the brown.

How to apply concealer to under-eye area: Use the synthetic brush. Concealer is highly pigmented and should be applied sparingly. Evenly distribute under the eyes with dots, then pat and blend up to the eyelashes.

How to apply to red spots: What this does is neutralize the red with a yellow base color. Use the synthetic brush. Dot the product on each red spot. Take the tip of the pointed brush and feather the edge, blending out onto the skin. Leave the center alone.

Foundation

Foundation helps even out your skin tone, protects the skin from the environment and provides the perfect canvas on which to apply your lasting, natural-looking makeup. Foundations today have improved greatly and should be undetectable when applied correctly.

Choose a formulation according to your skin type: Dry skin requires creams or creamy liquids. Oily skin requires powder-based or oil-free liquids. Normal skin can use water-based, powder-based or oil-based formulas.

How to apply: using your sponge, pat along the jawline to match the neck, then work up. Gently stipple over the concealed areas so as not to move the corrective product. Use the back of your sponge to blend over the jawline, or back to the hairline. Tip: Squeeze water through the sponge first if you want a sheer application of a liquid. However, a damp sponge with powder will give a more opaque coverage.

Highlighter

This is a step many women leave out because they do not understand how to use it properly to benefit their facial features. It's magic! It comes in a cream formulation, usually in a pot or in a wand form. Whichever you choose, you will need to use your synthetic brush to apply it in strategic areas of your face. Again, it is highly pigmented. Use a very small amount.

What it does: It reflects light. By placing it in the shadowed areas, it magically lifts out the shadows, giving an even look to the skin.

How to apply: start by looking where the shadows are. If your eyes are close-set, put a dot on the inner corners of the eyes along the sides of the nose. I always put a dot on the outer corners of the eyes to add brightness and a lift.

Under-eye bags can be diminished by placing highlighter in the indented areas.

Check the laugh lines and paint a faint line next to and above the crease, then blend up. Look at the sides of the mouth and dot where you see a shadow. It works!

Loose Powder

Powder gives a long-lasting, soft finish and prevents the foundation from moving due to the skin's secretions of sebum throughout the day. With the application of loose powder all your corrective products should look like they disappeared. Loose powder also lays the base for the blush to go on softly. Carry a pressed powder compact in your purse for your touchups.

How to apply: use your powder brush. Dip it into powder and tap off the excess. Then start on the outer parts of the face, ending with very little on the eyes. Press it in with your powder puff, folding the puff like a taco and using a rocking motion as you press the powder into the foundation.

Blush

The purpose of this magic step is to give a healthy, natural glow to your skin. It brings focus to your eyes. It can also bring drama to your face fashion.

How do you find your one basic color? Look at your natural lip color. Match that color or go slightly darker or brighter.

How to apply: using your blush brush, pick up the color on your brush and press it inside the brush with a tissue. Place the brush on your cheekbone at your hairline, then pull it forward toward your nose. Stop under your eye. Blend in circles.

Eye Color

For basic classic eyes, start by dusting your eyelids all over with a natural-looking pale shade that blends with your skin. This is to even your skin color and absorb any oils on the lid, which will now assure a well-blended, soft appearance to the colors you add.

Add a deeper color along the crease and blend. Next, take your accent color to the outer corner, pressing your applicator to the eyelid, then stroking inward toward the middle of the eye. After all colors are put in place, blend up toward your eyebrow with the blending brush.

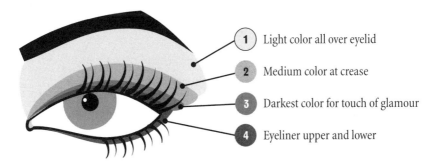

1. Light color all over eyelid
2. Medium color at crease
3. Darkest color for touch of glamour
4. Eyeliner upper and lower

Eyeliner

For a daytime look, eyeliner should be soft and subtle. This can be accomplished either by using your angle brush to apply a darker eye shadow along the lash line, or with a soft pencil, blending out the line with a cotton swab. Evening calls for a wider and darker eye line.

Eyebrows

Your eyebrows form the frame for your beautiful eyes. I recommend that they never overpower the eyes in any way. A delicate tweezing and slight lightening of the brows should do it. Fill in color only where needed, with emphasis on the arch.

Lips

After age 25, a woman looks great with a more defined lip line.

Use a neutral color lipliner or one that matches your lipstick. To make your lips appear fuller, slightly overscore the lip line. It must not be obvious.

If you have a lip line challenge, I encourage you to find a concealer pencil the color of your skin and lightly run it around your lips. Blend into your foundation, then start your lip liner color. This technique also helps eliminate "bleeding" into fine lines.

You can look polished with a classic red lip, a simple pair of black slacks and a white blouse. It is amazing! Aren't we glad to be female?

Yes, your most beautiful years are yet to come! Beauty is an ageless process. Practice on one part of your makeup at a time. Persist until it becomes easy and you will find a polished look that is uniquely yours. Remember, practice makes beautiful.

BARBARA LAYNE, PhD
Academy of Makeup & Fashion

(818) 905-0828
info@ladylayne.com
www.makeupandfashion.info

$\mathcal{B}$arbara Layne, founder of the Academy of Makeup & Fashion, offers professional classes to assist aspiring image consultants and makeup artists in developing careers in the ever-expanding fields of fashion styling, beauty and media makeup artistry.

Building on twenty years of experience internationally as an independent film, television and print makeup artist, Ms. Layne also created Star Image to assist the entertainment industry in developing and packaging talent. Over the years she has had the privilege to work with hundreds of top Hollywood talents, including Florence Henderson, Jeff Goldblum, Phyllis Diller, Teri Garr, Pat Boone, Sally Kellerman, Heather Locklear, Connie Stevens, Sharon Stone, Dennis Hopper, Leslie Uggams, Debbie Allen, Mimi Rogers and many more.

Barbara enjoys teaching and motivating others, as well as passing on the secrets of making the most of personal resources to develop an individual's self-confidence and self-esteem. She finds it personally rewarding to help in launching the careers of budding fashion consultants and makeup artists, and derives great satisfaction from enhancing others' personal style.

Secrets of a Stylish, Yet *Savvy* Shopper

How to Shop Smart to Save Time, Money and Stress

By Milena Joy

The ultimate style goal of any woman is to have a wardrobe she loves. You do not need to have a uniquely creative fashion sense or an unlimited budget to look great. Developing smart shopping habits will help you attain the right clothes that work for you and make you feel amazing. Here are ten of my step-by-step secrets on how to shop like a pro to save time, money and stress.

Secret #1: Be in the Know

Before you even think about stepping into a store, you need to know what you have and what is missing from your closet. Depending on the time of year, focus on your spring/summer or fall/winter wardrobe. Try every piece of clothing on and use a critical eye to see what fits and what is worn or is just simply outdated. Remove those pieces from your closet. Write down what needs to be replaced or what items you could add to create additional outfits.

You are now ready to create a shopping list. This is a long-term list of things that you need to fill the gaps in your closet. Review your calendar and take note of upcoming events, like weddings and holidays that may require the purchase of a new outfit. You will want to include these items on your shopping list so you are prepared when the day comes. Just like you should never go to a grocery store hungry, you should never go to the mall needing to find a dress or special event outfit at the last minute. By planning ahead, you will walk out with something that is not just okay, but spectacular!

Secret #2: Look the Part

When you are ready to hit the stores, put on an outfit that says, "I'm a savvy shopper!" I suggest to all my clients that they put on a cute pair of jeans, a tank layered with a shrunken blazer, and some flats for a look that feels comfortable, yet pulled together. Whatever you decide to wear, make sure it makes you feel good. You will have a better shopping experience if you are in a good mood. That is also why sales associates often will compliment you on something you are already wearing. You are more likely to buy something when you feel good.

A study on the effects of dress proves that dressing in a stylish and attractive manner will also get you better service and treatment at the stores. "How well-dressed you are is one indicator of your status, and how much money you have to spend," says Sharron Lennon, co-author of the study and professor of consumer sciences at Ohio State University. "Salesclerks believe that a well-dressed person is more likely to buy, and that affects the treatment she receives."

Remember to wear the appropriate undergarments. Think about what you will be trying on. If you are shopping for summer clothes, wear a nude bra as summer clothes tend to be lighter and thinner. If you are planning on trying on cocktail dresses, you may want to bring along a strapless bra and your favorite body slimmer.

Secret #3: Go Solo

We often think of shopping as being a team sport. However, when you really need to get something accomplished, like finding a dress for that wedding in two weeks or finding the perfect pair of jeans, challenges like these are best done in the company of no one. Having friends or your children with you is a major distraction or provides an excuse for you to give up too early on meeting your goals for the day.

Even if you are not under pressure to find something, friends may try to talk you into something you are not excited about because they like it or it fits their style. Your friends can also prevent you from trying new things because they think it is not "you." If your goal is to try new things and get out of a style rut, then that is the whole point. When you shop alone, you do not have to answer to anyone and it is all about you.

The only things to bring with you on your shopping trip are:

- **Shopping List.** This will keep you on task to walk away with the things you need.

- **Orphans.** Those items in your closet that you do not wear because they are missing the right shoes, the right top and so on. Bringing them with you saves a lot of guesswork and time.

- **Snacks and Water.** You are likely to need some fuel along the way. I always book my shopping appointments with clients for 12:00 noon or 1:00 p.m. so they have had at least one or two good meals to hold them until dinner. This also saves time so you do not have to break for lunch.

Secret #4: Try Before You Buy

This goes without saying—you actually need to try the clothes on before you buy them. Every brand fits a bit differently and sizes are not always consistent, even within the same brand. This alone is a great reason not to be married to a size. It will save you a lot of time if you try clothes on now, rather than waiting until you get home. If you wait until you get home, you will not be able to easily switch out the size without making another trip to the store. You will also run the risk of forgetting about the return and ending up with a piece that does not fit.

I encourage you to try on everything that catches your eye. Instead of holding it up to you and trying to decide at the rack if you should try something on, grab and go try on whatever sparks your interest. Clothing always looks different on. There is only one way to find out if it is the right piece for you. If you are buying pants or jeans, you will often need to try on several before finding that perfect pair. It sounds like a daunting task, but once you are undressed in the dressing room, it is easy to just slip in and out of several things.

Always ask a sales associate for help in getting different sizes. It will save you time in getting dressed again. If they do not have the size you need, ask if you can order it. This is possible at many stores and they will often ship it to your home for free!

Secret #5: Keep Your Eyes on the Prize, Not the Price Tag

"A bargain is something you can't use at a price you can't resist."
—Franklin P. Jones, American businessman

This is probably the best-kept secret of a savvy shopper, and may also be the most challenging one for you to follow. The price tag is often the culprit behind why you have all those clothes in your closet that you do not wear (some with price tags still on) or that do not fit quite right. It is easy to get charmed by sales or discounts and find yourself buying things only because they are on sale.

I always coach my clients to look at the price tag after they have tried something on. Once you are in the dressing room and have made your selections, look at the price tag and decide whether or not it fits into your budget. If it does, hurray! If not, then you can always let the sales associate know you are interested in the piece and she can notify you when it goes on sale. Then it will be a true bargain— something on sale that looked great and fit perfectly.

Focus on the quality of the clothing rather than the price. This may cost you a bit more in the short term, but will save you a lot of money in the long run. Higher quality clothing will almost always cost more. That doesn't mean you need to buy only expensive things. What it does mean is that you should be willing to spend a little more for a higher quality fabric that will last longer than cheaper fabrics that may wear and tear much more quickly.

Pay attention to seams. Are there loose threads or does the fabric look like it will easily pill? If so, it is probably not very high quality. Does the pattern align at the seams and does the fabric feel smooth and soft? These are both signs of higher quality and design. Make these evaluations a habit and you will only purchase clothes that look great and fit well.

Secret #6: Know Your Budget and Buy the Best You Can Afford

Although we would all love to be able to buy whatever we like and not be hindered by price, reality must set in at some point.

Frequently, we do not have a clear idea of what we spend or should be spending on our clothing. Here's a quick exercise you can do to start mapping out your budget:

List all your clothing items you intend to purchase on a sheet of paper. Next to the list of items add two columns labeled Minimum and Maximum. For each piece, think about how much you would realistically expect to pay for each item. Then, take the items on your shopping list and put the corresponding minimum and maximums next to each item. Total up the minimums and maximums and this will give you a realistic range for your budget.

Allocate more of your budget to spend on classic pieces, which will stay in style longer than trendy pieces that go out of style quickly. Next, calculate the cost per wear. The more often you wear an item, the less it actually costs you to wear it each time. Take a pair of $150 denim jeans, as an example. You can wear the same jeans several times in one week. In comparison, if you rarely wear a dress, except for special occasions, then you may only get a few wears a year out of a $150 dress.

Secret #7: Buy Only What You Love

Sounds simple enough. If you buy only things you love, you will only have a wardrobe filled with clothes you love. When you are in the dressing room and you have found a few pieces that look great on you and meet your budget, your next qualifying criteria is, do you love it? Whether a piece is five dollars or five hundred dollars, only buy it if you truly love how it looks and feels on you.

Instead of blankly staring into your closet every day, wondering what to wear, you will instead be overwhelmed with delight in choosing which favorite outfit to wear next!

Secret #8: Stick to Your Color Palette

Be wary of only buying the colors you love. I once had a client who had an entire wardrobe of soft, cotton-candy pinks. Literally ninety percent of her wardrobe was pale pink. After doing a color assessment where I analyzed the colors that looked best with her skin tone, we found that baby soft pink was not her color; frankly, quite the opposite. While I would not discourage someone from ever buying something that was not ideal for their skin tone, I would recommend that no more than ten percent of your wardrobe should fall outside your ideal color palette. If you do not know what your ideal colors are, then make an appointment with an image consultant who specializes in color. The effect color has on your complexion and the overall look and feel of your outfit will truly amaze you.

If you buy within your color palette, you will find that it will be easier to mix and match pieces within your wardrobe. I like to keep color very simple and have my clients focus on warm colors versus cool colors. Once you arm yourself with at least that much knowledge, you will be on the way to having a cohesive wardrobe.

The overwhelming choices in clothing will also become more manageable when you know what colors work and which ones do not. Combing through a department store, you can avoid certain racks all together and just focus on clothing that matches your color palette.

Secret #9: Relax at Home and Shop Online

Savvy shoppers know that some of the best deals are available only online. On the plus side, you can shop in your pajamas. On the downside, you may have to deal with returns and sizing issues. Here are some easy tips to make the best of your online shopping experience:

- **Search for discount codes.** In your search toolbar, just enter the name of the store you want to shop plus the term "discount code". You will be presented with a list of sites that offer you different discount codes for special savings at checkout at your favorite online stores.

- **Price compare.** If you find a great pair of shoes that are a bit out of your budget, check online to see if they are on sale anywhere. Brick and mortar retailers will often match any offer you see online. If not, do not be afraid to buy your item online from a reputable site.

- **Join email lists.** Many stores now have weekly or daily email newsletters with special sale announcements. Chain stores often have special online discounts that are not available at their brick and mortar counterparts. Also, many sales often hit the online store before they hit the retail store.

- **Shop online stores that have brick and mortar locations.** Ease the hassle of returns or exchanges by buying online and returning unwanted items to the retail store. You will save on return postage fees and will likely be able to get the right size right away.

Secret #10: Learn From Your Mistakes and Your Successes

"Anyone who has never made a mistake has never tried anything new."
—Albert Einstein, German-American physicist

Your shopping experience should be a day filled with trial and error. Moving out of your comfort zone is your guide to discovering or refining your personal style. If you have bought things in the past that did not work, write down the brand, size or any details that will prevent you from making that error again. Likewise, keep a journal of brands, stores and the details of things that worked. Was there a sales associate who was really helpful? Keep her name and number in your address book for next time.

If you have a habit of buying clothes and not wearing them, add a pop-up reminder to your calendar for the final return date. That way, you will not be stuck with an item that you will never wear, and it will also serve as a reminder for you to wear it. Always keep the tags on your clothes until you actually wear them, so if you decide to return them, you can. Chances are that you are not really in love with a piece if you have not worn it and the return deadline has arrived. In that case, just return it and get something you love instead.

Putting It All Together

We are creatures of habit, so it may take you some time to make all ten secrets routine. I encourage you to take baby steps along the way and adopt your favorite secrets first. As you begin to implement more of these ideas, you will not only see your wardrobe become more stylish, you will realize all the time, money and stress you have saved yourself. With a little discipline and commitment, anyone can benefit from these ten secrets and become a stylish, yet savvy shopper!

MILENA JOY
Milena Distinctive Image Consulting

Look successful. Feel successful. Be successful.

(303) 585-0589
joy@milenaconsulting.com
www.milenaconsulting.com
www.milenablog.com

*M*ilena Joy is a corporate and personal image consultant, professional speaker and author. She is the founder of Milena Distinctive Image Consulting, a full-service image consultancy located in Denver, Colorado.

Clients from around the globe, including Europe, Canada, California and New York, benefit most from her eye for style and her ability to harmonize it with their unique personality, preferences, body shape and lifestyle. She recognizes that what you see on the runway and in fashion magazines doesn't necessarily work for everyone. She excels at helping each client discover and create her own distinctive style!

Milena has been a featured speaker for such groups as Greenburg Traurig, STERIS and The Junior League of Denver. She inspires and motivates individuals to be the best representation of themselves and their companies. She teaches individuals how to strategically use their image to gain an edge in the workplace and to achieve their personal and professional goals. Her straightforward and insightful speaking style is empowering!

Milena Joy is a member of the Association of Image Consultants International, serving on her local board, and is a graduate of the Image Resource Center of New York.

Building Your *Perfect* Wardrobe

By Shirley Borrelli

*T*he Perfect Wardrobe Builder™ is a fundamental formula that strategically and specifically enables you to always have something to wear that looks well put together. It minimizes the number of pieces to maximize the number of outfits. It is a system that builds the outfits for you!

Each piece of clothing is carefully chosen to mix and match with all the other pieces of clothing in the wardrobe. These 11 pieces coordinate into 30, 40, or even 60 outfits. Imagine a month's worth of outfits with no repeats.

I always recommend my clients buy quality over quantity when building the perfect wardrobe. The aim is to buy individual pieces—rather than complete outfits—through strategic planning before purchase. The objective is to amortize the investment of your clothing per outfit, and then per wear. For example, say you purchased a wardrobe for $1000. Divided by 30 outfits, this equals $33.33 dollars per outfit. Assume you will wear these outfits 12 times. (Once per month for 6 months, for 2 seasons = 12 times). $33.33 divided by 12 = $2.78 per wearing. That's more-than-affordable shopping and you will always look well-put-together.

Understand that building your perfect wardrobe takes an investment in a few well-chosen pieces instead of buying stand-alone outfits when you need something to wear. Buying an outfit without consideration to its mix and match potential guarantees a closet full of clothes and nothing to wear.

Your perfect wardrobe can be built upon with the addition of new tops with patterns or with sweaters, vests or wraps. Consider jazzing up your wardrobe with accessories before adding new pieces. Jackets, cardigans and vests are considered the third piece that will give any outfit instant polish and style.

The Perfect Wardrobe Builder Formula:

2 jackets
5 bottoms
+ 4 tops
———————
30+ outfits
All pieces must coordinate
with each other

2 Jackets (considered a third piece)

• Choose a basic neutral color like black, grey, or white.

• Could be a cardigan, vest, pashmina or blazer. At times, a V-neck sweater could serve as your third piece.

5 Bottoms

Depending on your lifestyle, you may need all jeans, all skirts and dresses, all pants or a combination. The following are suggestions to get you started:

• 1 dress pant; straight leg, flat front, mid-rise

• 1 dark denim jean; straight leg, flat front, mid-rise

• 1 knee-length skirt in a cotton blend

• 1 knee-length skirt in a more formal fabric or suiting fabric

• 1 party dress

4 Tops

Most wardrobes need a ratio of three tops to one bottom. This wardrobe builder is a beginning.

• 1 turtleneck (for the small-busted) or a V-neck sweater. Choose a fine knit.

• 1 button-up collared blouse/shirt in a color that repeats your eye color. Choose cotton fabric for daytime, or satin for more elegant daytime or evening wear.

• 1 cotton T-shirt (V-neck or scoop neckline)

• 1 tank top (wider straps) or camisole (spaghetti straps)

Once you have 11 pieces of clothing that coordinate with each other, take any one jacket, any one bottom, and any one top. Voila! An outfit!

The Perfect Wardrobe Builder automatically makes an outfit by choosing one garment from each of the three categories in the formula: 1 jacket, 1 bottom, and 1 top = one outfit.

Accessories

Accessories will change the look of the outfit. Add a belt, purse, necklace or scarf; earrings, bracelets; even hair adornments. Try layering more than one necklace or bracelet to add interest and style. Avoid wearing matching earrings and necklace; it can be too contrived and lack interest. Consider adding a hat to your inventory of accessories.

Unfortunately, accessories are often overlooked items in a wardrobe, yet are essential to looking polished and stylish. This is where your personality needs to shine! Rather than wondering what accessories "match" your clothes, choose accessories that attract you and that you will enjoy wearing! Start with these basics:

- Metal band watch for your career or dressier occasions
- Leather or canvas strap watch for leisure and sport activities
- Medium hoop earrings or studs on French wires
- Single pendant necklace

For more tips on using accessories, see Dominique Vaughn-Russell's chapter, *Accessory Challenge!* on page 105.

Shoes

The shoes you wear are an important accessory. They need to be functional yet attractive. No frumpy shoes, please! There are many styles that are comfortable and fashionable. Here are seven basic shoes you need in your wardrobe to take you through all four seasons:

- Polished flat heel (less than one inch). Consider walking the mall in these shoes. Try a loafer or ballet flat.
- Heeled shoe, with a minimum two-inch heel. For evening, choose a metallic/strappy shoe.
- For business, choose a pump, slingback or peep-toe.
- Athletic shoe for physical activities.
- Flip-flops for walking to the pool, beach or around your hotel room.
- Flat boot for cool weather to run errands.
- Heeled knee-high boot to wear with denim, pants or skirts. For colder, snowy climates, buy one size larger and add a thermal insole for extra warmth. Ask your shoemaker to add a rubber sole and replace the tip of the heel with rubber. Essentially, this will make your boots less slippery and provide more functionality. Try a wedge boot. Try stretch fabric if you have larger calves.

Bags/Purses

Typically, you will need:

- A tote bag
- Daytime purse with straps to hang from your shoulder that is not as big as a tote bag
- An evening clutch

Outerwear

- Belted trench coat for breezy, cool, rainy days
- Fall wool-cashmere blend jacket that falls mid-thigh
- Winter down-filled parka with hood

Winter Accessories for Colder, Snowy Climates

- Thermal-lined, leather driving gloves that come past your wrist bone. Consider an exciting color rather than black or brown.

- A toque or snow hat that provides head and ear protection from the cold. There are many stylish options available at clothing stores or department stores.

- A long, cozy, knit scarf to tie in a hacker knot. Choose any exciting color that flatters your skin tone. This is not only a stylish option, it is also warm and toasty!

- Opaque tights that match your knee-high boots.

- Knee-length trouser socks. Look for a wool blend for added warmth. White cotton sport socks should only be worn with athletic shoes.

The Perfect Business Wardrobe Builder Formula

For your professional wardrobe, buy the best quality you can afford. These jackets and bottoms are your fundamentals, and quality pieces will serve you very well. Follow this formula and you will always look polished. This will also work well when travelling for business.

add:
bright print scarf
high-heeled boot

add:
multi-strand
long necklace
flat boot

add:
pump shoe
choker necklace

add:
strappy shoe
clutch bag

I highly recommend you buy as many pieces as possible at the same time from the same clothing collection to ensure optimum mix and match possibilities.

- Suit pant; you may want to consider two pair of pants: one hemmed for heels and one hemmed for flats
- Cocktail-length skirt in a fabric suitable for evening wear
- Knee-length skirt: A-line, straight or pencil, preferably in the same fabric as the jacket
- Sheath or one-piece dress

2 Jackets

- Suit jacket; button fastenings are more polished than zip closures.
- Less structured jacket, yet still professional. This could be a cardigan or suit-fabric vest. Perhaps choose a softer color yet still a neutral. Consider a different fabric with texture, a luxurious pattern, a bronzed metallic or a soft velvet.

5 Bottoms

- Pant #1: same fabric as the suit jacket; flat front, straight leg (not tapered), mid-rise, hemmed for your daytime heel
- Pant #2: hemmed longer for your evening heel. Best if it is the same pant as #1
- Cocktail-length skirt: choose an evening fabric. This gives an opportunity to wear boots or polished ballet flats for day, then a metallic, strappy heel for evening
- Knee-length skirt: the same fabric as the other pieces in the suit. Try a trumpet, A-line, straight shape or pencil skirt, depending on your body type
- Sheath dress: same fabric as the other pieces, if possible. This dress can take you from boardroom to an evening event by changing

accessories. Therefore, keep the design simple and form-fitting to your body without being tight. If you are unable to find one, it is worth having one made.

4 Tops

- Crisp white or off-white, button-up collared shirt. Buy the best quality you can afford. The collar needs to hold itself up to frame the face and give instant style.

- Softer fabric, button-up blouse in a bright color or perhaps a print with your flattering colors. Repeat your eye color for instant pop. This blouse usually has an interesting neckline.

- Cotton white or off-white T-shirt. Look for an interesting neckline: V-neck or scoop. Pay attention to the seam on the neckline; it should be neat and clean. No men's undershirts, please!

- Camisole/tank top with straps wide enough to cover your bra strap. You need to be able to remove your jacket without feeling exposed or inappropriately dressed for the office.

Shoes

- Two-inch or higher pump for pants, sheath and knee-length skirt

- Polished ballet flat. This is a lower-heeled shoe that is comfortable enough to walk the mall, yet looks good with pants or a cocktail-length skirt

Bag/Purse

- Leather briefcase. Consider one on wheels—it leaves your right hand available to open doors and shake hands. It never looks professional to use shoulder straps.

- Small purse that you can take out of your briefcase when going for lunch, to the ladies' room or out to dinner. This purse should comfortably accommodate your personal ID, debit/credit card, lipstick, mirror, breath spray, facial tissue and feminine protection without bulging.

Jewelry

- Nothing that jingles or jangles; this is too distracting at the workplace. It can annoy your colleagues.

- Clean, simple, metal designs work best. Sentimental, fine jewelry may not have enough presence for your professional wardrobe. Consider a statement necklace of the finest construction.

Watch

- Buy the best quality watch you can afford. Diamonds are not necessary.

- Consider an Eco-Drive watch by Citizen®. They never run out of batteries.

- Choose a face size and shape that complements your body frame size. A larger woman should not wear a small-faced watch.

Hosiery

- It is a must in the professional wardrobe. Bare legs instantly suggest a more casual, loose and relaxed attitude or approach. Bare legs may be stealing your credibility.

- Wear trouser socks with pants.

- Opaque tights. Avoid bright, neon colors in the workplace, unless you are in your 20s and work in a creative industry.

Overcoat

- Choose a knee-length coat in the best quality you can afford.

The Perfect Casual Wardrobe Builder Formula

Some casual pieces can mix and match with your business wardrobe to create a business casual wardrobe that would be appropriate for work. Casual fabrics include cotton, cotton blends, linen, denim and synthetic fabrics. Save yoga wear for your leisure time. It does not belong at the office.

2 Jackets

- Statement jacket in an interesting fabric, color or pattern
- Cardigan sweater in your flattering color
- Other jacket options are a windbreaker, jean jacket or a leather or suede jacket in your eye color

5 Bottoms

Choose bottoms that will take you from a chilly day to a warmer day. The variety in bottoms will provide you with the perfect mix and match possibilities.

- Dark-wash denim jeans, mid-rise. Pant length is key—buy a longer length to wear for casual evenings out with boots or heels. Pay attention to back pockets: do they lift or drag down your buttocks? Flap pockets tend to be the most flattering on most body profiles.
- Buy a second pair of jeans to wear with your flats or walking shoes. Hem should be 1/8" from the floor. Never wear athletic shoes with denim.
- Chino or cotton-twill casual pant: neutral color; darker for colder months, lighter for warmer months. Wear with a low heel.
- Knee-length cotton skirt: A-line or trumpet, must look more casual and playful than your suit skirt, with a soft, flowing, movable feel.

- Cargo pant: this is a very casual, leisure-looking pant—no ironing required. Wear with flats or lower-heeled wedge shoes.

4 Tops

Most of these tops will be cotton or a cotton blend. Look for fabrics with some stretch to keep them comfortable.

- Cotton, button-up shirt with collar. Soft color in a solid or pattern. Could be used as an outerwear piece or worn over a tank, under a jacket or sweater or alone. This will be a key piece in this wardrobe. Keep it pressed for a crisp look.
- V-neck, fine-knit sweater. Consider a solid neutral color for the most mix and match possibilities.
- Cotton layering tank: be sure the straps are wide enough to cover your bra straps. Choose fun colors to bring playfulness to your outfit. Length should be long enough to cover your waistline and peep out from underneath another top.
- Three-quarter-length-sleeve, cotton T-shirt with embellishments on the neckline. Colors in a print should pick upon the same colors as your layering tank tops.

Shoes

These must be comfortable, yet stylish.

- Lower heeled or flat (think comfort/walking); for example, a ballet flat or wedge heel.
- Sandal (this is not a sport sandal); wear with casual skirts.

Bag/Purse

- Choose a shoulder bag that is large enough to carry all your "stuff," plus a water bottle. Make this a fun bag.

Accessories

• Have fun with style, shape and color. Choose accessories that resonate with you. Try a leather watchband. Choose a larger-faced watch to keep it more exciting and playful. Layer costume jewelry for fun.

These Perfect Wardrobe Builders are the basic foundations to build outfits effortlessly to have you dressed stylishly for a variety of occasions. No more dashing to the mall looking to buy an outfit because you have somewhere to go. This formula prepares you at a moment's notice to always have something to wear by creating a wardrobe strategically. You need to carve time out of your schedule to build it. Dedicate 15 minutes every Saturday morning to declutter your closet and pare down to the essential pieces that coordinate with each other. Or, plan an hour to pull the 11 pieces of clothing and create a wardrobe. Memorialize your strategic wardrobe by taking a picture of each 11-piece wardrobe you build. Then build a head-to-toe outfit from that wardrobe to include accessories. Take another picture. Continue building outfits and taking pictures from the same 11-piece wardrobe. Use these pictures for inspiration for what to wear for effortless and stylish dressing. No stress. You are ready at a moment's notice because you've created a wardrobe that serves you. You've created complete outfits. You are in control of the clothes! You will prove to yourself that you will have the perfect wardrobe and always have something stylish to wear.

SHIRLEY BORRELLI
Image Consulting

(780) 451-0661
info@shirleyborrelli.com
www.shirleyborrelli.com

*S*hirley Borrelli is a passionate educator who brings more than twenty years of experience in training, writing and consulting to her image and personal branding company. Shirley authors and publishes *Image Boosters,* articles and booklets on image, personal development and communication skills. Her most recent book publication, *Clothing 101,* reveals an exclusive formula to build The Perfect Wardrobe™, lists the top ten ways to stress-free shopping and the benefits of color analysis.

Shirley is a regular contributor to the media and has appeared on Global TV, Access TV and City TV. She has been featured in numerous provincial and national publications. She is the producer of *Edmonton Makeovers: Look Years Younger.*

Shirley is a certified image consultant with the internationally recognized London Image Institute in image, professional development training and personal branding. She is a certified personal color analyst with Sci\Art Company and is a member of the Association of Image Consultants International. Shirley graduated from the University of Alberta with a bachelor's degree in Education and a major in Business.

Your *Personal* Proportionality
Solving the Perfect Fit Puzzle

By Teresa McCarthy, AICI FLC

$\mathcal{A}$s a petite woman, I have had trouble getting a good fit even though I have always shopped in petite stores. Although sales staff would assure me that the clothes looked wonderful on me, I often left the store with a sinking feeling. I knew that even though I had settled for the best that was available, it just wasn't a perfect fit and it seemed unlikely that a seamstress could actually do anything with it to make me feel really good in it.

Then I met someone who had similar figure challenges but who had undergone a wonderful process of discovery that provides for her, for me and for all who are interested, a near-magical solution to our problems. But it is not magic. It is the application of a mathematical formula to our skeletal frames. I am excited to have this opportunity to share this knowledge with you.

Clothes Talk

No matter where you go or what you do, your clothes speak volumes about you—and they had better be saying the right things. Clothing is part of what people judge when they form a first impression. In the first four minutes of an encounter, people form up to 90 percent of their opinion about you. They will make at least 25 judgments about you, including your age, income, education, authority, friendliness and trustworthiness, what kind of car you drive and what kind of house you live in.

With this in mind, you owe it to yourself to try not only to be the best you can be, but to be confident in the knowledge that what you are wearing stands for what you are all about and, most importantly, that it fits.

Image Spoilers Relating to Fit

The most expensive garment you can purchase loses its great look if it does not fit you properly. Some commonly encountered problems are:

- **A sagging bust**—never underestimate the importance of a well-fitting bra. No matter how wonderful an outfit looks on a mannequin, avoid disappointment by having a professional fit you for a good bra before you try that outfit on. Many department stores and some specialty stores have professionals on call to assist with this very important purchase. The bra, after all, is the foundation for your excellent fit.

- **Uneven or drooping shoulders**—shoulder pads are part of a posture fix. If you stand in front of a mirror and see that your shoulders appear droopy, investing in shoulder pads can make a substantial difference in the way you look. These pads need not be thick, but what they can do to improve the look of an outfit is truly amazing. In the event that one shoulder is lower that the other, you might try two pads on the lower shoulder to balance it with the other.

  Sometimes, the shoulder pads in a structured jacket seem too large. If that is the case, the collar will stand out from the back of your neck and creases may appear in the shoulder area. Instead of removing the pads completely, ask your tailor to insert thinner pads.

Shoulder pads can create the illusion of taking as much as 15 pounds off your figure and 15 years off your age. You can find them in most department stores and fabric stores.

- **The too-tight look.** Tugging at your blouse or jacket to keep it from gaping or to get it back into its proper position is not only uncomfortable, but draws attention to an area that will now appear larger. Sometimes, all you need to do to remedy this is have your tailor sew on an invisible snap in the bust area.

- **Uneven hemline.** Sometimes, the tummy protrudes, causing the hemline to ride up in the front. Conversely, a protruding posterior can cause the hemline to be up in the back. Be sure to have your hemline measured all around while you have the garment on. It is also important to check that the lining does not fall below the garment.

Fit Guidelines

- **Skirt.** It should not be too tight or too short—do a sitting test check. A pencil or straight skirt should not ride up more than two inches when you sit. Pockets should remain closed and not pull open, and material should remain loose around the body.

- **Pants.** They should drape smoothly over the body. There should be no baggy areas that droop or tight areas that pull. Check the pocket lining for smoothness. Avoid panty lines.

- **Jacket.** It should also drape smoothly. Generally, the best length for sleeves is to the wrist bone. If a long-sleeved blouse is worn underneath, the polished look is to have the blouse cuff extend one-half inch below the jacket sleeve. The collar should lie flat and not wrinkle across the back.

- **Shirt.** To ensure buttons do not pull, leaving a gap, there should be enough fabric on each side of the bust to allow for an adequate amount of give. The fit of the shoulders depends on the style of the shirt.

- **Clothing scale.** Know your body shape and try to find clothing that reflects that shape. It is best to stay away from clothes that are too tight, but baggy is not the best look either.

Body Shapes

There has been much written about body shapes and it is important that you know your body shape. Here are the names of the different body shapes.

- **The Hourglass or Figure Eight.** It is curvy and well-balanced, small-waisted, with hips the same width as the bust. The waist should be emphasized in this figure, and the use of belts helps.

- **The Triangle, A-frame or Pear Shape.** The body is narrower at the top half and wider at the hip and upper thigh area. Wearing lighter clothing on top with shoulder pads or sleeve detailing can help balance this figure.

- **The Inverted Triangle, V-frame or Diamond Shape.** The shoulders and bust appear wider than the hips. Usually the waist is shorter and the hips high. Wearing garments that have width and fullness in the skirt or pants will help widen the hip area.

- **The Oval or Apple Shape.** Most of the weight is carried in the front of the body and the waist is larger than the hips and bust. Clothing should be flared and drapable and flow loosely over the waist. It is usually desirable to have skirts and dresses fall at the knees.

- **The Rectangle or H Frame:** With age, the Hourglass or Eight Frame sometimes morphs into a rectangle. In some cases, the bust and hips remain in proportion but the waist expands into a

Contoured Rectangle, with only slight indentations at the waist. The waist should not be the focal point, and belts are not recommended. Darts also help to contour an outfit. The complete absence of a waist indicates the Rectangle. The sides of the body will now become close to a straight line; straight skirts and jackets are the best fit. Belts should be avoided.

For more about dressing for your body type, read Lisa Ann Martin's chapter, *Shapes of Style,* on page 81.

Linear Proportionality—The Perfect Linear Figure

Leonardo da Vinci possessed one of the greatest intellects in history. His insatiable curiosity led him to explore the dimensions of the human body and develop his Theory of Perfect Human Proportions. He incorporated this into his 1490 drawing and text entitled *Vitruvian Man* in tribute to a Roman architect called Vitruvius Pollio. In about 25 AD, Vitruvius put forth his theory on universal human proportions. Leonardo was not the only one to highly value the work of Vitruvius; it had been studied by artists for 14 centuries.

The drawing by Leonardo and the accompanying text are often referred to as the Canon of Proportions. The *Vitruvian Man* remains one of the most referenced and reproduced artistic images in the world today.

Essentially, Leonardo's theory was that the perfect male human figure stands eight heads high. I will not go into a discussion of variations on his theory—for example, the fact that Michelangelo, who painted the Sistine Chapel between 1508 and 1512, disagreed on the location of the mid-point of the human frame. He put it at the leg-torso joint as opposed to the crotch. Most artists agree with Michelangelo on this point, but still revere the genius of Leonardo.

The key thing we must learn from these great pioneers in knowledge is that there are certain ideals of human proportion few of us can measure up to. Our awareness of this leads us to recognizing the need to get beyond the discussion of the ideal or perfect proportion and into examining the imperfect.

Going from Perfect Proportionality to Personal Proportionality

Janet Wood Cunliffe of Annapolis, Maryland learned about Leonardo da Vinci's Theory of Perfect Human Proportions through her study of clothing design and art. It was during an art course that the theory suddenly took on new meaning and importance.

Janet drew out her own figure and compared it to the perfect figure, eight heads tall. A "eureka moment" occurred! It was suddenly clear to her that manufacturers can produce clothing which is a perfect fit for a perfect figure because they know the measurements that have been agreed upon as perfect. For those who do not fall into that category, including herself, Janet knew that she must find a formula that would guide her and others to a perfect fit, by examining our skeletal structures individually.

The Fashion Fit Formula® (FFF)

The formula itself is a proprietary piece of intellectual property which Janet developed, consisting of a series of mathematical calculations and algorithms. It is based on Leonardo da Vinci's theory, which states that the combination of head, torso and legs can only have eight horizontal divisions to provide perfect balance. It is based also on the Divine Ratio of the Fibonacci Sequence of Numbers, or a ratio of 1:1.618, which is found throughout nature. This is also known as the Golden Mean.

The formula is applied to any individual's unique frame by taking twelve vertical measurements of the *pivotal points* of that person's skeletal structure, from the top of the head to the ankle. Those measurements are then fed into a computer program which applies the Fashion Fit Formula (FFF) to provide for that individual a personal guide—her unique solution for a perfect fit.

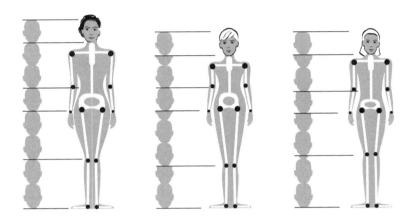

Just as each snowflake has a unique structure, so do we. Each person's bone structure is unique. In the above illustration, the first figure represents a perfectly proportioned linear figure, eight head lengths tall. The second and third figures represent real women (actually, Janet and her business partner, Kathy McFadden) who are both five feet, two inches tall.

Note the differences in their bone structure. Notice the short torso of the second figure as compared to the first and third figures. The second figure also has long bones from the hip to the knee when compared to the other two women. Assuming the women wear the same size clothing, they would look like the figures below, wearing the same dress with different results.

From your skeletal measurements, the FFF proprietary software generates a unique solution for you. In all cases it gives guidance as to the specific lengths that should be applied to various pieces of clothing so the clothing falls at your proportional points, creating an illusion of balance.

Most image consultants are aware of the Golden Mean, have been trained in vertical proportions and can suggest ways to compensate for less-than-perfect proportions. The FFF can provide additional information to assist with this process.

Guidance Provided by the FFF Applies to:

- Jacket lengths: cropped, short, standard, above-knee
- Skirt and dress lengths: micro-mini, mini, street, mid-calf
- Shorts and capri lengths: short-shorts, Bermuda shorts, long and short capris
- Sleeve lengths: above and below the elbow
- Perfect neckline point
- Adjusted waistline and belt widths

Tips to Complement the FFF Personalized Solution

- **Necklines.** If your face is round and your sweater or dress has a round neckline, before you decide there is no help for the look, experiment with a necklace or scarf. If you place it at your perfect neckline point, it leads an observer's eyes from that point up to your eyes, making them the focal point, giving you a more open look. If your necklace is shorter than it should be, perhaps you could add an extension.

- **Sleeves.** There is a perfect three-quarter-length point as well as a short sleeve point. Provided the jacket and pants or skirt are the same color, by pushing sleeves to the three-quarter-length point, you create a break in color as well as reduce one layer of material, causing the abdomen and hips to appear less wide. Hemming sleeves on a slant will create the optical illusion of a smaller waist (short sleeves) or hips (three-quarter-length sleeves).

- **Waistlines.** The natural waistline is rarely at the right point to create balance on the torso. The FFF effectively chooses an adjusted waistline, either above or below the natural waistline, to create the illusion of balance. It is up to you to decide if you wish to emphasize your waistline. If your waistline is proportionally large in relation to your bust and hips, take special care not to unnecessarily draw attention to it.

The Value of Your FFF Solution

Since each body is unique, no two FFF solutions are alike. Each is completely customized to the client's vertical dimensions. It creates symmetrical balance in clothing and will provide the illusion of a perfectly proportioned linear figure. The measurements are accurate to 1/8 of an inch. Since the formula is based on vertical measurements, it is independent of weight gain or loss and lasts a lifetime.

Your FFF solution will pay you back many times over. It will help shop wisely, avoid bad buys and will give you the confidence to buy garments you like and know you can have altered to fit you perfectly.

Shopping in Your Own Clothes Closet

Using your own FFF solution, you can personally, or with the help of an image consultant, go through your clothes closet and reassess the clothing you have not been wearing. First, decide if the color is right for you and if a little tweaking can change the look of the garment enough that you would truly enjoy wearing it. Then, you can weigh the merits of investing in the cost of alterations versus buying an alternative new garment.

Clients I have worked with are amazed that for a small investment in alterations, they have been able to bring back to life outfits they had given up on.

Availability of FFF Solutions

FFF solutions come in two versions: an email version and a Just The Facts version, which contains a laminated solution to take shopping and a 15-page booklet, filled with information and tips. You can also be totally in charge and measure yourself, following instructions provided on the FFF website, www.fashionfitformula.com

Whether you obtain a personalized FFF solution or not, put more attention on fit and use the many tips discussed in this chapter to ensure you look your best every time you get dressed. After all:

It's not what you wear . . .

but how you wear it!™

TERESA McCARTHY, AICI FLC
Image Solutions Group

It's not what you wear . . .
but how you wear it! ™

613-724-1030
teresa@isginfo.com
www.imagesolutionsgroup.ca

*T*eresa McCarthy believes that "you are what you have chosen to become," but also that your persona is partly inherited. Her mother was recognized as a wonderful teacher who (surprise!) always looked her best.

Looking good and performing well, and helping others to do the same, come naturally to Teresa. Appearance is only one of the characteristics she helps others to improve. She is a founding partner of Image Solutions Group, Ottawa, Ontario. Their corporate motto includes, ". . . by looks and acts and what you say, your *image* is left behind." Good appearance must be accompanied by good behavior and good communication— both verbal and nonverbal.

Teresa's passion is helping others to increase success potential. She holds certificates in fashion modeling, in public speaking and in Special Education from McGill University. She is a member of the Association of Image Consultants International, whose program of continuing education she values highly.

She has conducted training in the government, corporate, educational and non-profit sectors, is active in numerous community organizations, and has received very favorable television, newspaper and magazine coverage. She authors a regular column in *Fifty-Five Plus*, an award-winning magazine.

What Do Your Glasses Say About *You*?

How to Have Them Say What You Want

By Michele Bayle, LDO

We spend a lot of time getting ready in the morning. You pick out your outfit, choose the right shoes and do your hair and makeup. Then you put on that same old pair of glasses and head out the door. Many of us don't consider glasses as an important part of our image. How many times have you put off getting new glasses? How often have you just bought the cheapest pair of reading glasses from the drugstore? Eighty percent of us need some kind of eye correction, so why is it that most of us don't really care what our glasses look like?

Many people feel that shopping for glasses is a chore, it takes too much time or you never know what looks good on you. My goal is to show you that choosing the right glasses can be fun—it does not have to feel like a chore or be boring. I'll share some shopping tips to help you make a good eyewear purchase. By the end of this chapter, I want you to go from settling for a ho-hum pair of glasses to finding a great new pair that excites, fulfills and defines you.

Putting Your Best Foot Forward

Your face is the first thing people see. I am sure you have heard that we only have an instant to make that first impression. Actually, opinions are being formed about you and your product and/or service within the first three seconds. You cannot afford to miss a beat with those first impressions, and there are many opportunities for them every day.

Think about how you make your decision to do business with someone. If one thing about a person is off—a spot on the shirt, dirty glasses (one of my pet peeves), hair that looks too messy or un-styled, clothing that does not fit properly—we begin to judge them negatively. Do not let this happen to you. As you pay attention to the professional details of your life, please do not overlook the impact eyewear can make.

My client, Julie, came to me looking to replace just the lenses in her existing frame—not an unusual request. Julie's frame was about five years old and beginning to look a little dated. Julie works in the software industry and tries to sell her clients new upgrades that she knows will help their businesses thrive, even though her clients can be a bit resistant to change. She loves her job and knows her product inside and out, but was having trouble making her sales goals.

I suggested to Julie that we try a little experiment. "Julie," I said, "you are selling the latest and greatest in software and technology, but you are not keeping up with the latest and greatest for your own personal image. Sometimes we need to dress the part to complete the presentation. How about considering a pair of glasses that will boost your confidence and gain the respect of your clients?" Julie agreed it was time to update her eyewear.

We picked out a fantastic plastic frame that I would describe as classic with a twist. Julie has an oval-shaped face, so we chose a rectangular shape in tortoise with green on the inside. She looked great and was excited to take her new look for a test drive. Two months later, I received an email from Julie telling me she landed a *big* sale and attributed that to the boost of confidence she got from her new glasses.

Choosing the right pair of glasses can make you look more professional. It can make a young person look older—if she were in a position typically held by someone with more years and needed to look the part. It can make an older person look younger and seem more competitive, cutting edge and youthful.

Make Sure People Fully See Your Personality

Have you ever thought that the most sensible thing to buy is black? It will go with everything, right? Wrong. I bet you are thinking you need to play it safe with your eyewear because you are an accountant, or a lawyer or a (fill in the blank). But that black wire frame is not always the best choice. When you are seeking a new client, especially one on the cutting edge of anything from fashion to technology, playing it safe may be a bad thing. You are giving them the impression that you are old-fashioned and "square." Black can equal safe, but it can also say that you lack creativity or expression. You have to think about your ideal client. The under-45 crowd is very in tune with trends and appearance. If your clients are in that age range, you need to branch out from basic black.

I recently had a client who was wearing a silver rectangular metal frame; a pretty unobtrusive selection that partnered well with his conservative attire. I would actually go as far as putting the glasses in the boring category. Dan owns a marketing company. He is great at what he does and thinks outside the box for his clients. Dan called and said he needed a new pair of glasses and wanted something similar to what he already had. We met, discussed his business, and I told him I felt that his glasses did not match his personality or his business. His glasses were boring, while his personality is creative and fun. I fit him with a frame that was a classic Malcolm X style, but with some pizzazz and with light blue on top. Larger than his other glasses, these frames brought out his blue eyes and made him feel a little more progressive and innovative.

It is important to express who you are with your eyewear. For example, if you are an accountant who enjoys playing the bass guitar with your weekend band, it's okay to have a little fun with your eyewear. So how do you do that? Perhaps the shape of the eyewear you choose is traditional, but the plastic has texture or color to it. Think of the texture of clothing and the colors you typically wear. Adding an element of that to your eyewear will finish off your look intentionally. It is like putting on a necklace or picking the right pair of shoes to complete your ensemble.

Choices Galore!

Nowadays, you have a plethora of products from which to choose. Glasses come in many styles, shapes and colors and they can say a lot about a person. When shopping for eyewear, you will find many options of materials, ranging from titanium and stainless steel to plastic and combinations in between. Color and texture are applied to metal in many ways and at times can even look like plastic, with all of the bright colors and treatments. Some of the newer plastic frames have many layers laminated together to provide texture, color and pattern to create a three-dimensional look. Recently, I saw a beautiful pair that had a piece of fabric laminated between two layers of plastic. With all these options, make sure to play around a little bit with your eyewear selections.

Some people wear frames that disappear on their face. This might be a rimless frame or a frame where the color matches the skin tone, and it is hard to tell where the glasses start and end. I call this style of eyewear "quiet;" it is almost as if the wearer does not want anyone to see the glasses. When choosing a pair of glasses that disappears, be careful that the result is not aging and the shape is complimentary to your facial features.

Some people choose glasses specifically to be bold and out there. I have a client whose favorite color is purple. She drives a purple Volkswagen, most of her clothing is purple and of course we always choose a purple frame for her. Being bold with your choice of eyewear tells people you are comfortable with who you are. Embrace your uniqueness!

Personally, I have a classic style, but occasionally like to dress on the funky side. I have a couple of pairs of glasses that work when I am being conservative; each with a subtle color, but not your basic black, brown or tortoise. When I am in the mood to dress a little more artsy, I wear a pair that has about six different colors tastefully partnered into one dramatic frame. When I wear these glasses, I get the most compliments. People *like* to see others in glasses that do more than just correct their vision, but also suggest something more about who they are. Getting these compliments will boost your confidence and encourage you to express yourself in other ways, too.

Tips on Finding a Great Pair of Glasses

The first thing you should do before trekking out to find the perfect pair is to think about how you use your glasses. Not only in what you do for a living, but how you use them in your spare time. Do you play sports in them? Do you do a lot of close-up work, such as reading or knitting? Are you outdoors a lot for work or play? Keep all of this in mind when you start shopping.

Elements and principles to remember:

Skin tone is important. You do not want to choose a frame that will bring out too much red in your skin tone, making you look flushed or sunburned. We all have the ability to wear red successfully, but take a careful look at what it does to the skin tone when you try it on. If you have red undertones in your skin, stay away from cherry. Go with a brick red. Cherry reds will complement darker skin without making it appear red. A more olive skin will look good in brick reds. People with pale skin should choose something more on the raspberry side.

Hair color can change. Don't make this an important factor in choosing your eyewear. The cut, color and style of hair changes frequently, especially for women. However, the glasses should still work. If you have longer hair, bring a hair clip with you when shopping and pick something that works with your hair both up and down.

Enhance the color of your eyes with your selection. If they are blue, this can be done by selecting a blue frame; however, make sure the shade works with your skin tone. Green eyes can be enhanced by a green or a deeper, more denim blue. You can add a little sparkle to honey-brown eyes with a plastic frame that has some gold undertones to it.

Consider the positioning of the glasses on the face. Does the frame cut your brow line off? We communicate with our brows, so don't cover them up. Your glasses and eyebrows should not be competing.

Pay attention to the shape of your face. If you have an oval face, select a frame that has a bottom on it, rather than a rimless frame. This line break will balance out the length of your face. Be careful with round frames, and stay away from the drooping round glasses, which will elongate your face. Go with a more angular frame that will bring out your cheekbones.

For a round face, a frame that has angles in it will take the place of invisible bone structure, thus creating angles and balance of line. Another option for round is a modified cat's eye which will create a slimmer face. A definite no-no for round faces is a round frame.

A square face should stay away from sharp edges; soften your face with a circular frame or a frame with a soft shape on the bottom and a more dramatic line across the top. This will give the jawline a softer appearance and draw your eye upward, minimizing the square jawline.

Heart-shaped faces or the inverted triangle shapes should consider a frame that is wider at the bottom than at the top. This shape will balance out the more prominent chin line. Soft curves are also a great look for the heart-shaped face. Just remember your goal here is to minimize the width of your cheek bones.

The width of the frame is important, too. Regardless of the shape of your face, you do not want to have your glasses wider than the widest part of your face. That might be the cheekbone area, the jawline or even the forehead. Also, keep in mind how centered your eyes are in the frame—you want them in the center of the lens area.

The depth of the frame, meaning from the top where the brow line is to the bottom under the lower lid, is really important. If the frame is too deep it can have a drooping effect on the eyes, making the wearer look older or sleepy. In a world where we are always desiring to defy age, this one is crucial. There is a fine line between a good fit and one that is too deep.

Beyond Style and Color . . .

Some additional tips to keep in mind when shopping for your new eyewear: Make sure that the glasses are not resting on your cheeks. If you have a small bridge or high, full cheeks, choose a frame with adjustable nose pads to keep the frame off your face. Play against your facial contours, and don't be afraid of trying color.

Your lenses are an important part of your professional image, so don't stop at the frame. I always recommend anti-reflection lenses for a few reasons—they reduce computer screen and nighttime road glare, and images are crisper, because you don't have to fight with the white light dancing across the lenses. Also, when people look at you, they can see your eyes and not be distracted by the dancing white light.

If your prescription is substantial and your lenses are thick, select a high-index lens. This will make your lenses thinner, lighter and prettier. Stay away from tinting the lenses with a cosmetic tint. Tinting your lenses a slight gradient pink or blue just puts a barrier in front of you and your client or customer. If you want the appearance of makeup, I recommend choosing a frame with some color instead.

Along with the style, the care you give your glasses needs some intentional thought, too. Make sure your glasses are clean, properly adjusted and in good repair. Glasses with a piece of tape or paper clip holding them together will definitely give the wrong first impression. A reputable optical store can adjust or repair your glasses for you if you are not near the place where you purchased them.

As you shop for glasses, have fun exploring the possibilities of style, color, shape and texture. Remember, a great pair of glasses will boost your energy and confidence!

MICHELE BAYLE, LDO
Wink Eyewear

The eyewear store
  that comes to your door

(206) 676-2624
michele@wink-eyewear.com
www.wink-eyewear.com

According to Michele Bayle, owner of Wink Eyewear and eyewear industry consultant, the right pair of glasses has the power to transform who you are. As a licensed optician with more than 19 years of experience, Michele believes that the impression you make—and the success you achieve—has a lot to do with what your glasses tell others about you. Want to look younger, without investing in an expensive surgical procedure? Glasses can provide a solution. Want to seem playful, intelligent, more sophisticated, artsy or reflect more of your secret inner qualities? Think glasses again.

Michele's talent for helping you explore the many sides of yourself and mirroring back what works is what makes Wink Eyewear, an innovative, mobile eyewear business, so successful. Serving discerning clients across the Western United States since 2007, Michele offers a wide selection of designer eyewear to help you express more of who you really are. Her greatest satisfaction comes from the self-confidence she inspires in her customers. In addition to her mobile retail business, Michele also owns Wink Optical Solutions, a consulting service that provides customized practice solutions for optometrist and ophthalmology professionals.

Cultivating Your *Authentic* Style from the Inside Out

By Deborah Reynolds

Defining Your Authentic Image

*H*ave you ever asked yourself the following questions: "Who am I? Who do I want to be? How would I define my image, my sense of fashion and style? How can I authentically convey who I am through my appearance and behavior?" These are important questions worth pondering. Defining your image will help you achieve success in your life. How I define success will be different from how you define it, because we are different people with different goals and aspirations for our personal and professional life.

> *"Success is not to be pursued.*
> *It is to be attracted by the person you become."*
> —Jim Rohn, American motivational speaker, author

That means that rather than spending time chasing after the illusion of success, it is more effective to focus your time and energy on building yourself into someone who is worthy of admiration and respect. In the process of developing yourself, you will find that you naturally succeed because you recognize and attract successful people, events and opportunities. This may seem counter-intuitive, but it is the most efficient way of creating what you really want in your life. Why waste your life endlessly chasing after what you want, only to have it slip from your grasp? By focusing on developing your character, you will begin to draw circumstances and others to you, like a moth to a flame. You will begin to want better things and a better life for yourself and those around you. You become the source that attracts what you want directly to you. Surround yourself with people who not only respect you, but who are willing to do whatever they can to help you attain your goals.

Your Outward Appearance Will Affect Your Behavior

When focusing on defining and improving your authentic image, I encourage you to start with your wardrobe and physical appearance. It's the quickest way to make a change. In a flash, you can go from looking slovenly to professional or to sensual and alluring. Check the fit and proportion of your wardrobe and make sure you have all the essentials covered. You'll find many more helpful tips on upgrading your appearance in the other chapters in this book.

If you change your wardrobe to make yourself look more beautiful, attractive, professional or approachable, it might improve your attitude for a little while, but eventually you will revert to your old ways unless you change your perspective, what you value, your behavior and ultimately how you think. To maintain your exterior change, first make sure that there is a strong authentic character foundation to support those changes. If you begin from the inside and work your way to the outside, the changes will be realistic, will be based on who you are, will reflect an image of who you want to become and, more importantly, will be easier to maintain.

Here is what you can do right now. First decide what kind of person you are and want to be, both inside and out, and make the changes you need to project and become that person. It's natural to want to start with your personal image and then create a professional image for the workplace. Having a competitive edge will instantly set you apart from your competition and make you more memorable. It's essential if you're in the dating scene and you and a few other women are trying to attract the same man. It even works the same if you are competing for a promotion.

Follow some of these core principles and you will not only find long-term success in your career, but in your personal life and relationships. Wouldn't it be wonderful to have people wanting to be around you because they recognize you as a person of quality—an exceptional woman who stands out in the crowd? Having a well-pulled-together image and a good reputation goes a long way towards getting you noticed, known and remembered . . . for all the right reasons.

Being in business since 1990 has taught me to guard my image and reputation closely. I make sure that everything I wear, do and say demonstrates that I am a person of quality and integrity, and that each wardrobe piece is designed to send a congruent message. Are you in touch with what your image says about you? Here is a way to get clear. Think about your image and what it means.

What is Image?

In the dictionary, image is defined as:

- The opinion or concept of something
- The character projected to the public
- A mental picture
- A vivid representation
- An expressive or evocative representation

Image comes from the Greek word *imago,* which means *I am.* Deep down, each of us has the occasional concern or even fear that we may not be well received. We want to be liked for who we are, without conditions, but sometimes we find ourselves trying to live up to others' expectations of who we should be, rather than being authentically our best selves. By pretending to be someone other than who we really are, we dishonor ourselves and rob others of the chance to get to know us. By hiding our true selves, we foster a lack of respect for who we are, which further diminishes our self-esteem and confidence. "I am" is a powerful declaration of your authenticity. But declaring "I am sad," "I am worried" "I am depressed," I am unable to…," "I am incompetent" or "I am stupid," is also powerful and dangerous. Thoughts are things. Be careful what you wish for and be careful what you declare.

Think about your very best authentic self—imagine the best of what you have to offer and are capable of—and emphasize your full and complete potential. I suggest writing out one hundred affirmations about who you are and clarify who you want to become as a person. Complete the statement, "I am…" and read it twice a day. Here are a few to get you started: I am beautiful, I am confident, I am positive, I am powerful. The process of writing and reading affirmations is not only life-enhancing and life-changing—it is pure magic!

Image is a combination of your belief systems, how you see yourself in your mind's eye, and what is out there in the world, blended together with your personal experiences. Each element adds color to your image. Many of us see others from a very superficial standpoint. We look at what they are wearing, how they act, the type of people with whom they interact, and we make judgments based on what we see. If we were to expand our awareness of others, we would have a much richer experience of who they are. Rejuvenate all your relationships and take the time to really know the people in your life. Who do you want to have a conversation with and get to know better today?

Image affects everything—and everything that you do affects your image. The way you look affects how people treat you, the way you feel, the way you think, your perceptions, attitude and the way you behave. Change one aspect and you affect them all.

When assessing a client's image, I look at the whole person—who she is, what she represents and the roles she plays in her life, such as wife, mother, daughter, divorcée, single and dating, career woman or volunteer. I also look at what she believes in, what nuances she demonstrates and how she sees herself. I do not evaluate her on appearance alone. Image is so much more than that. I am looking for a demonstration of character, intelligence, likeability, charm, her personal perspective and whether she expresses it through her appearance. What are the characteristics or unique attributes you want to describe you?

Your Image Must Honor Your Authentic Self

You don't have to be afraid of showing your real self to others. Instead, accept and celebrate yourself by reading and reflecting on the unique attributes you have written down and find a way to celebrate the wonderful person you have become. This is the cornerstone to developing your personal brand. An authentic image is grounded in the very core of who you are. Who you are is a culmination of all your past experiences and decisions—good and bad. Enjoy the miracle and mystery that went into developing the masterpiece you have become, and use it as the foundation of an image can be proud of—one that will honor your authentic self and communicate it to the rest of the world. If you are a mother, imagine what a wonderful gift that would be to your children. If you are in a relationship, imagine that gift your partner will receive. If you are single, by being your best self, you will attract a fine partner worthy of you, if that is what you want.

You are always communicating. Whether you say the words or don't say the words, you are still communicating. Everything about the way you look sends messages to others about what your value is. Your body position, energy and facial expression subtly communicate who you are on an instinctual level. Take notice of how you are sitting or standing at this very moment. Shift your posture, put your shoulders back and take a deep breath as you smile. Notice the difference? You instantly feel energized.

If you want to be successful and have people take you seriously, discover what your image is silently telling others. The best image to create, whether you are dressing yourself or creating a company image or brand, is designed to:

- Reflect an awareness of first impressions
- Be an intentional, purposeful image
- Be appropriate for the environment, the occasion or event, the industry, the relationship or the client
- Reflect the best aspects of your personality, your life, your career, and/or your business
- Reflect your client, target market and industry
- Connect with your audience
- Create and build rapport
- Reflect the best of what you have to offer
- Be integral and ethical

- Reflect your uniqueness as you want to be noticed, known and remembered
- Focus on creating a great, lasting impression

Understand Your Image

How do other people see you? As noted earlier, each of us has the occasional concern or even fear about not being well received. We want to be liked for who we are, without conditions. In order to gain a better understanding of your image, ask yourself a few core questions. What do people really think about me? Do they think I am attractive, confident and polished, or unattractive, dumpy and disheveled? What message does my appearance communicate to others about who I am? Does my total image express what I want it to express? Am I unconsciously expressing an image that creates a faulty perception of who I am or is my image sending mixed messages?

From a business standpoint, if a potential customer walks into a store or business, the visual component is a prominent factor in the image he or she sees. Is the environment visually pleasing? When you invite a customer or business associate into your office or a guest into your home, do you and that person feel comfortable and at ease? Does your environment reflect your overall image? How we do anything is how we do most things. It's all interconnected.

Others see us as an overall package. It includes who we are on the inside, what we look like on the outside, how we care for ourselves, in what environment we work and live, the state of our vehicle and how we care for the items we own. Our world is made up of the places we work, play and live. They reflect who we are and what our inner state is. Take a quick assessment of your appearance, your office, your car and your home. Are you proud of your personal appearance and of your home and office? Any shame or embarrassment we might feel affects our overall confidence and self-esteem. Take ten minutes a day to shift your environment with decluttering and increased organization. Upgrade your appearance with a new hairstyle, a fresh manicure, a crisp white shirt and a fabulous pair of shoes.

If you are unsure if you come across the way you intend, ask a few of your trusted friends and colleagues. Most of us don't really know what others think of us, so be sure to approach competent, confident, intelligent and positive people for an opinion. It takes a lot of courage to check in with people and find out what they really think. In order to move from where you are now, uncover the confusion and establish a clear understanding of where you are currently.

You Have More Power Than You Realize

Maybe you're single and want a great guy in your life. If you want a wonderful partner, you have to first be a wonderful partner. If you want to be perceived as sensual and attractive, you have to become a sensual and attractive person—inside and out. It is attitude as well as appearance. If you want a good, grounded, reliable husband, you first have to become a good, grounded, reliable wife. Quite simply—like attracts like. Are you the type of person who is worthy of a promotion at work? Do you possess the people skills and leadership qualities to inspire others to follow you? For you to be a leader, people must be willing to follow you. You are not a leader if you have to force or coerce people to do what you want. Are you the type of person who deserves to be voted into office or sit on a board? You first need to have the characteristics to lead and mentor. You have to become to get.

All decisions in life are based on our core values. If you have trouble making decisions in your personal or professional life, it might be time to get clear about your core values. My core values are loyalty, commitment, integrity and trust. Here is a partial list of values. Which values do you want to live by, each and every day?

Adventure	Enjoyment	Joy	Recognition
Awareness	Excitement	Kindness	Respect
Balance	Flexibility	Leisure Time	Security
Capability	Focus	Loyalty	Self-Discipline
Caring	Freedom	Maturity	Service
Commitment	Generosity	Motivation	Success
Confidence	Grace	Nurturing	Thankfulness
Creativity	Happiness	Passion	Tolerance
Dependability	Health	Peace	Understanding
Discipline	Imagination	Power	Variety
Energy	Integrity	Prosperity	Wisdom

Brainstorm about what you want to achieve over the next six months personally, professionally, health-wise, financially, emotionally and spiritually. By designing your life with a solid plan, you will have a much clearer idea of the image and style it will take to achieve your goals. Once you are aware of which elements of your image and style need to be developed, you will be in a position to build a life that will get you noticed, known and remembered for all the right reasons. Plan your image development rather than leaving it to time, luck or circumstances, and success will come easier and faster than ever before.

There is a reason why you are reading this book. Perhaps you're desiring to enhance your personal life, your career or your business. Take a leap of faith and transform yourself and your life. Take a moment to jot down a few notes about how you can change your thinking, your belief systems, perspective and attitude, and how you can manage your emotions a little differently to feel good about yourself. Consider more self-control, discipline, focus, and being intentional about how you portray your image. It's about time you were on the receiving end of the wonderful gift of transformation. Figure out what is not working, get inspired to fix it, and move on to create your own unique style for the rest of your life. It's time to get noticed, known and rememberedfor all the right reasons. Being who you are and projecting your authentic self through your image looks good on everyone.

DEBORAH REYNOLDS
About Face Image Consulting, Inc.

It's important to create a good first impression, but essential to create a great lasting impression!

(604) 888-9260
info@aboutfaceimage.com
www.aboutfaceimage.com

*D*eborah Reynolds is a sought-after international image expert, speaker and business consultant. She is a contributing author of the bestseller, *Wake Up . . . Live the Life You Love: Living in Clarity,* and is the author of the soon-to-be-released book, *Getting You Noticed, Known and Remembered: Building Your Business Image From The Inside Out.*

Having captured one of "America's Most Wanted" and one of Interpol's Most Wanted as an Immigration Investigator, Deborah brings the same passion and drive to her business. Deborah started her business in 1990 as a professional makeup artist, and the company has evolved to include image enhancement services, corporate training, consulting and speaking. She has worked with such companies as the Pepsi Bottling Group, B.C. Hothouse Foods and Halsall Engineering. Deborah takes a unique approach to enhancing, refining, repairing and branding your personal, professional and business image. The process starts by helping her clients establish clarity around how they think, who they are, their core values, and character, style and image development. A no-nonsense but approachable businesswoman, Deborah is an action- and results-oriented image expert who gets her clients noticed, known and remembered…for all the right reasons.

Looking Great at *Any* Age

By Alison Vaughn

*W*e live in a world of Botox® and personal trainers, of liposuction and Lipo in a Box®. The rule to "dress your age" is no longer relevant. Age 50 is the new 40, 40 is the new 30 and 30 is the new 20. So what does this mean for you? If you are 50, do you have to buy skirts that hit below the knee or can you wear that mini-skirt that still fits and looks good? If you are in your 20s, is it okay to wear Doc Martens with baby doll dresses? Your image depends on how your life age works with your personal style. The more the two are in harmony, the more together your image.

> *"Style is knowing who you are, what you want to say and not giving a damn."*
> —Gore Vidal, American author

Dress for Your Life Age and Personal Style

Your life age isn't just about your chronological age; it includes how you look, act, think, feel and much more. This is the age you want to represent through your personal style.

Do you know women who are in their 60s, but look closer to 40? They do not just look young; they act young and think young. Do you know women who are in their 30s, but look, act and think as if they were pushing 50? Sure you do. They probably look closer to 60 than 50, too. A woman wears her life age like a garment. It says more about her than she could ever say with words. What is your life age?

Your personal style is how you present yourself to the world. Your personal style gives you confidence and communicates volumes about who you are and what you value. It comes from the choices you make about apparel, accessories, demeanor, gestures and so on. Your career, social status, marital status and apparel choices influence your personal style but should not dictate it.

Who you are and what you do must be considered when you make choices about what to wear and how to conduct yourself. Does this mean your personal style must follow a set of rules dictated by others? Not necessarily. You just need to understand the effect your style has on others. When other people look at you, they make judgments about you based on what they see. Appearance creates a picture of who you are. If you are a pediatrician, your personal style on the job would differ from a kindergarten teacher. Both work with children, but each has a different image to present.

When other people lack personal information about you, they may use your personal appearance to judge your character. They may judge your ability and disposition by that first impression. Have you seen the film Legally Blonde? It is about a young woman whose boyfriend jilts her, so she follows him to law school to get him back. Once there, she discovers she is better at the law than he is. The humor in the movie comes from the contrast between the heroine's image and her profession. Perky, sassy, petite blondes who wear pink suits and carry a poodle do not fit the image of an attorney, so when she succeeds, you are surprised. While her image fits her life age and her personal style, it does not fit most people's image of an attorney.

Appearance can be a powerful and useful tool in controlling the kind of message you send to others about who you are, your age and how you view your age. If you get the response you want, your style fits; if you do not get the response you want, consider making some changes. By changing any part of your personal style, such as hairstyle, grooming or clothing, you can change the total image others have of you.

Universal Principles Create an Ageless Image

"Delete the negative; accentuate the positive!"
—Donna Karan, American fashion designer

When you ask people to name women with an ageless image, most name Princess Diana, Jackie Kennedy and Audrey Hepburn. These three women symbolize the perfect marriage of life age and personal style. Their dress was always age-appropriate whether they were dancing at a ball, walking down the street in New York or hugging a child in a poverty-stricken village.

How did they do it, and how can you do it, too? Here are seven principles of age-appropriate dressing these fashion icons can teach us no matter our age or personal style.

1. Clothing should always fit properly. Even if your body is in tip-top shape, too-tight clothing is rarely flattering and often is too revealing. On the other hand, baggy clothes make you look sloppy and unprofessional. Both say you do not care about the image you present to the world. Do not pay attention to sizes. Each label will fit you differently; you might wear a size 8 in Oscar de la Renta, a size 10 in Valentino and a size 12 in a bridal gown. Do not drive yourself crazy with sizing numbers. Always take two sizes into the fitting room and relax! Buy clothes that fit the largest part of your body and then have them tailored.

2. Choose shoes to fit the occasion. Mile-high stilettos work for after-work clubbing and parties, but extremely high heels are too sexy and inappropriate for the workplace. Choose the highest heel appropriate for the occasion. Going to work? Stay in the two- to three-inch range.

3. Jewelry is an accessory, not the entire act. There is nothing wrong with an armload of bangles or long, dangling earrings as long as they do not distract from your image. Limit accessories to fewer than five at one time, including earrings, necklaces, bracelets, watches and belts. Less is more. Choose iconic pieces that say something about your style and are appropriate. Pearls are never out of style—since Coco Chanel popularized them back in the 1920s and Audrey Hepburn took them to the big screen in the 1960s.

4. A little leg goes a long way. How short your skirt is depends on the condition of your legs. The shorter the skirt, the sexier you look—but only if you have the legs to carry off the shorter length. Can you wear a short skirt if you are in your 60s? Sure, if you have the legs and the occasion warrants it. While it is never a good professional move to wear minis to the office, skirts do not have to be ankle-length. Generally, keep them about an inch-and-a-half above the knee.

5. Avoid peek-a-boob looks. Except for lolling around poolside or in the privacy of your bedroom, there are few legitimate opportunities to show off your chest. It is especially important to avoid wearing low-cut garments to the office or for business functions. If you cannot part with your V-neck shirts, put a lacy camisole underneath. Save bare midriffs for the beach.

6. Dress from the skin out. Ever wonder why these iconic women always looked so put-together? Why their garments moved so smoothly over their bodies? It is subtle, but the right lingerie makes a big difference in how clothing hangs and moves. You will never find a photo of these women with visible panty lines. Never. Visible panty lines are a visual assault to everyone walking behind you. Wear seamless underwear or a thong. If your panty line is still visible, your skirt or pants are too snug; you need to go up a size.

7. When in doubt, wear black. While trends come and go, black never goes out of style. Pair the perfect black dress with a brilliantly colored pair of shoes or a brightly colored bag. Sometimes just black looks perfect.

Rules for Women Under Age 30

"I've always thought of the T-shirt as the Alpha and Omega of the fashion alphabet . . . The White T."
—Giorgio Armani, Italian fashion designer

Choose styles that are chic, swank, modern.

This is the time of life when you are still discovering who you are. If you are in your 20s, whom do you consider a style icon? Many younger women name Keira Knightley, Natalie Portman and Anne Hathaway. These young women understand and apply the universal principles described earlier, and they bring their own personal style to their life age to create a completely pulled-together image. What can you learn from them?

- **Let go of the collegiate look** and embrace an office-appropriate wardrobe.

- **Avoid very trendy looks.** Add a few trendy pieces to your wardrobe each season, but pair them with classic, timeless pieces.

- **Keep your youthfulness in mind.** Get rid of anything you wore as a teenager. You want to cultivate an image that suits a young adult, not an aging teen.

- **Begin to define your personal style** and choose clothing and accessories that reveal who you are and support how you want people to think of you.

- **Always wear clothing in which you feel comfortable** and that is true to yourself. The purpose of fashion is to make you look and feel great.

Rules for Women Between 30 and 50

"The difference between style and fashion is quality."
—Giorgio Armani, Italian fashion designer

Choose styles that are flirtatious, attractive, sophisticated, adventurous, alluring, stylish, confident.

Women in their middle years usually name Sarah Jessica Parker, Heidi Klum and Michelle Obama when asked about style icons.

These women not only apply the universal principles, they have the confidence and self-esteem to occasionally break the principles. Sometimes it works; sometimes it does not. However, even when it doesn't, their image is never boring. They have panache. What can you learn from them?

- **Periodically review your style in relation to your life age.** Avoid being stuck in what worked for you ten years ago. Your body has probably changed since your 20s or 30s. You have different social, marital, parental and business responsibilities that need to be considered when making apparel choices.

- **Keep your wardrobe up-to-date by reading style magazines.** You do not need to recreate your wardrobe each season, just add a few new pieces in new colors that work with what you already have. First Lady Michelle Obama blends high-end and off-the-rack styles to create her own ensembles of powerful femininity.

- **Invest in quality pieces you can wear year after year.** This is the time when you settle into a career and begin to establish yourself. Choose a quality suit with coordinating pieces that include pants, skirt and jacket. This versatility will allow you to create many outfits using three staple pieces.

- **Take an occasional risk.** You are never too old for ruffles or polka dots, as long as you do them correctly, and it is appropriate for the situation.

Rules for Women Over 50

"You can only perceive real beauty in a person as they get older."
—Anouk Aimee, French actress

Choose styles that are elegant, dignified, dazzling, radiant, confident.

Older women are no longer relegated to black and navy wool dresses that hang down to their ankles. Nor do you have to dress like TV comedy icons such as *The Golden Girls* or Granny from *The Beverly Hillbillies.* Keep an image in mind of a person whose style you admire. Style icons for older women include Helen Mirren, Michelle Pfeiffer and Sharon Stone. Would Helen Mirren wear a Christmas angel sweatshirt? Maybe, in the privacy of her home, surrounded by grandchildren. In public? Never!

These women celebrate their bodies by their choice of clothing. They do not cover up their bodies; neither do they flaunt them. They dress to accent the positives and minimize the negatives. What can you learn from them?

- **Choose garments that make you feel confident and feminine.** Rather than showing it all off with short skirts, hint at the legs underneath by choosing a skirt with a provocative slit.

- **Wear timeless styles that transcend trends** and make a statement about who you are at this time of your life.

- **Avoid anything that draws attention to the waist** unless you have great abs. Generally as women age, muscle mass decreases, and the middle expands. Redirect the eye away from the middle. The easiest way to do this? Do not tuck your shirts in or wear belts; they emphasize the belly.

Rules You Need to Break

Like many things in life, some rules about dressing come from an earlier time. When you follow these rules, you seem older than your life age, so feel free to break them whenever and wherever possible.

- **No white after Labor Day makes no sense.** If white is a good color for you, wear it whenever you can.

- **Shoes and bags must always match.** Too much "matchy-matchy" makes you look grandmotherly. Even if you are a grandmother, do not dress like a stereotype.

- **No sleeveless tops for older women.** If you have good, shapely arms, flaunt them.

- **No sequins before dark.** If the occasion warrants sequins, wear them, regardless of the time of day.

Do you have fashion rules you cling to? Do they make you seem older than your life age? If so, stop following them. To paraphrase legendary fashion designer Coco Chanel, fashion is a matter of proportion. No matter which part of your body you find objectionable, there is always a clever way to divert the eye. The key is to use fashion to your advantage to give you the look you want, whatever your age.

Create Your Perfect Image at Any Age

Begin to create your perfect image at any age by reviewing the following list of adjectives.

Poised	Glamorous	Pageantry
Precious	Adorable	Gorgeous
Quaint	Gleaming	Graceful
Shiny	Colorful	Grotesque
Sparkling	Cute	Homely
Strange	Dark	Magnificent
Ugly	Drab	Misty
Tomboy	Distinct	Old-fashioned
Unsightly	Beauty	Plain
Attractive	queen	Blushing
Average	Unusual	Bright
Beautiful	Adventurous	Clean
	Aggressive	

Reflect on your image now:

- Think about your clothing and accessories and circle the adjectives that describe your current image.
- Do these adjectives take into account your life age and personal style?
- If not, what changes can you make to bring your image into alignment with your life age and personal style?

What you want your image to be:

- Put an "X" next to the adjectives that describe what you want your image to be.
- Do these adjectives take into account your life age and personal style?
  · Go through your wardrobe and accessories with your list of what you want your image to be.
  · Eliminate anything that does not support your desired image.
  · Begin to replace items with ones that are closer to the image you want for yourself.

Take this fashion inventory every year on your birthday and update your wardrobe to look great at any age. Begin to collect photos of styles that "speak" to you and start a folder of clippings. Review your clippings frequently, especially when you are shopping for clothing.

Always purchase the best quality garments you can afford and invest in classic styles, with trendy pieces added for accent. Focusing on your personal life age and style will help you create the image you want and will fill you with confidence and pride.

ALISON VAUGHN
Jackets for Jobs, Inc.

Changing lives, one suit at a time

(313) 579-9160
avaughn@jacketsforjobs.org
www.jacketsforjobs.org

*A*lison Vaughn is the Founder & CEO of Jackets for Jobs, Inc., a nonprofit organization that provides employment etiquette, career skills training and professional clothes to persons seeking employment. Since opening the doors in 2000, the organization has assisted over 10,000 individuals. This high-profile organization has been supported and applauded by Donald Trump, ABC's *The View*, NBC's *Today Show* and Oprah's *O Magazine*. A highlight of Alison's career was the distinct honor of ringing the closing bell for NASDAQ.

Alison received a bachelor's degree from Michigan State University and graduated from The Women's Campaign School at Yale University, sponsored by Yale Law School. She is a member of the Association of Image Consultants International (AICI), Distinguished Women in International Service, Top Ladies of Distinction and Gamma Phi Delta Sorority. She is the recipient of many awards, including the Humanitarian Award from Top Ladies of Distinction, Women of Excellence by the *Michigan Chronicle*, and Entrepreneur of the Year from Alabama A & M University. Alison is a former model, Miss America Petite Pageant contestant, *Jet Magazine* Beauty, Auto Show model, and was a High School Homecoming Queen.

Special Occasion Dressing
Lights—Camera—Action!

By Mari Bowlin, FFS

*A*re you ready to be the star of your life? The time for that special occasion has arrived. Are you feeling confident and assured? Or are you wishing you had a fairy godmother to assist you with knowing what to wear, when and where? Well, here I am to cast a spell of glitz and glamour!

Special occasions require us to have a sense of our unique, divine essence. Special occasions invite us to show up in a particular and spectacular way. Can you feel the pressure? No matter the occasion, the number one essential is to exude confidence. It is our most attractive feature. Let's start with identifying your unique, divine essence.

What's your style? You could be sultry, a goddess, girl-next-door adorable, glamorous, natural, an all-American beauty, boho, ladylike demure or a bombshell. Consider your motivation. Do you dress to be noticed—or to fit in? Is your number one criterion to be comfortable? Or is it important to express yourself in a creative, unique manner?

If you feel more confused and are in need of clarity, start with the exercise of going through magazines and catalogues and tearing out pages that resonate with you. Then look for common factors in terms

of color, style, fabric, pattern, texture and design. Next, shop your closet and seek out clothes that emit the essence of those characteristics. Think about the occasions at which you wore them and what worked, and where there exists a need for embellishment.

Are you inspired yet? Whatever the occasion, ask yourself what is it that makes it special? Are you a guest, or are you the guest of honor? Will all eyes be on you, or will you be one of many vying for the limelight?

Getting Ready

Start with an assessment. We all have features that set us apart. Some are genetically inherited while others reflect our self-care. The idea is to accentuate the positive and eliminate the negative. Take an inventory head to toe. We are opting for the art of illusion.

- **Hair.** Are you happy with the color, texture, cut and style?
- **Skin.** Look at the tone and coloring. Does your skin receive daily care plus weekly and monthly treatments?
- **Cosmetic Application.** Special occasions are opportunities to glam it up. Instant results can be obtained with the use of primers, illuminators, smoky eyes and red lipstick. Creating a brow that frames the eye is essential, as are both lipliner and eyeliner. For more tips on using makeup, see Barbara Layne's chapter, *Face Fashion* on page 139.
- **Grooming.** You want to be clean and fresh, of course, and you may wish to use fragrance to enhance your essence.
- **Body.** Fit and toned is the goal. An exercise program that incorporates flexibility, strength, and aerobics is key. We all feel better and certainly more empowered when we are fit and strong.

- **Also a must is a smooth foundation.** Fabrics that cling and silhouettes that hug the body demand smooth lines that are accomplished with the aid of shapewear. One of my favorite items in my wardrobe is a skirt made by Spanx. It combines the elements of shaper and skirt and is easy to pack. For more shapewear ideas, see Sandy Moore's chapter, *It's Not Your Grandma's Girdle,* on page 117.

This is the time to consider professional assistance for the gaps, be it a hairstylist/colorist, esthetician, makeup artist, or body trainer/fitness club. We are not going for perfection—more a sense of excellence as we strive to present to the world our most attractive self, and to ourselves, our most empowered and confident image.

Beauty Formulas for Special Occasions

There are so many opportunities for dressing up! Once you have taken care of the basics, you can focus on what to wear for each type of occasion. Use the following as guidelines, and add your own special touches.

Weddings

- **Bride.** How do you want to feel? Like a princess? Does every little girl grow up wanting to be swept away by a knight in shining armor, marrying the prince of her dreams? There are bridal shops galore vying to court you as you select the perfect gown. Attending bridal showcases can assist you in selecting those shops working with integrity. Because the showcases can be overwhelming, remember: the number one requirement when it comes to selecting a gown is that you love it. It needs to fit and of course it will be altered for your measurements if necessary. You have choices of many shades of white, ivory or pale pastels. And consider the embellishments—headdress and veil, gloves, pumps and so on. Add the things that express your divine self on this special day.

- **Bridesmaids.** Have they come a long way or what! My favorite option, given that all bridesmaids will show up as their unique selves anyway, is for the bride to select the color and skirt style. Each bridesmaid may then select a matching top in the style of her choice. Selections may include halter, off-the-shoulder, sleeveless, tank or princess style. This will ensure overall harmony, but with a sense of the individuals.

- **Showers.** A sheath dress with pearls is always appropriate and can be in a variety of colors, textures and fabrics. Even the pearls can vary in expression. One of my favorites is brown pearls with bronze beads and gold chains. This looks spectacular with a brown dress. For those preferring pastels and a more classic, refined and elegant look, the traditional white pearls in single, double, or triple strands will work wonderfully. For those wanting more punch, other colored pearls create a more distinct look.

- **Luncheons.** The mood will be celebratory and lighthearted. A dress is always appropriate for this occasion. A wrap dress is wonderful if that suits your figure. A silk shirtdress is another option. Choose a color in your eye color palette. If you are more comfortable with pants and that suits both your figure and personality, black or ivory pants may be worn with a myriad of tops. Think beaded tank, ruffles, patterns and the like.

- **Rehearsal dinner.** You may choose either a cocktail dress or pants in a fabric like silk or velvet, depending on the season. Wool crepe or any fabric that drapes or flows will project a message that says festive. One of my favorite looks—that feels fabulous—is evening pajamas.

Black Tie/Gala

This is the time to pull out all the stops. Sequins, feathers, fur and metallics are sure to dazzle. This may also be outfitted for the black tie evening wedding. These are the occasions where you may choose to wear elegant, dramatic black. Another stunning showstopper is to utilize color to create drama. Simply picking a color that enhances your eyes and going to the opposite on the color wheel with accessories will add punch and pop to your outfit. Combining colors in different ways creates different effects; remember the illusion and magic. We are casting a spell to express serenity, creativity, warmth, drama or refinement. Both long and short dresses may be worn. Silk chiffon or beaded halter-top gowns are good choices, as is sensuous silk. And don't be afraid to think outside the box if that approach is compatible with your intent. For example, Princess Diana stood out in a beautiful white lace gown in what was otherwise a sea of black eveningwear when she attended a gala in Washington, DC.

The Little Black Dress (LBD). Yes, it is a wardrobe staple and we may have many of them, considering this is an investment piece. The LBD can take you from the office to dinner and cocktails. For evening you may add a jacket, pumps and a clutch. Another time, try adding a belt, strappy sandals, pearls, lace and leopard to change the tone. For a real boho look, you can layer scarves and chains of belts, necklaces and bracelets. I add satin pumps, red lipstick and my mother's vintage bag and I am ready for anything with my "go-to" cocktail ensemble.

The thing to remember with the LBD is to recognize it in all its many varieties. That means finding the length that works best for your individual proportions. For example, if your legs are an asset, wearing the mini length is for you. Just remember balance; meaning, do not bare both the legs and arms. For those of you who have great shoulders, the one-shoulder dress is a fashion-forward look. It can either be sleeveless or one-sleeved. For those of you not ready for the drama of exposing one shoulder, consider an off-the-shoulder style. It is such a fabulous look that even Donna Karan has done designs for women whose arms have grown flabby, yet maintain the definition of toned shoulders. Strapless is another option, and it begs for a statement necklace. Keep in mind that all of these options may occur in various fabrics and textures.

Cocktail Parties

A slip dress in a great color and fabric will be a welcome addition to your special occasion wear. You may also choose the look of silk drawstring pants, glammed up with a spectacular blouse. Jewel tones, a statement necklace and a strapless top with a fur shrug create another look. One-shoulder asymmetry is unique and dramatic. Special occasions are also opportunities to deconstruct our daytime outfits for cocktail events. Adding a beaded or sequined top adds miles to an investment pant or skirt suit. You can even create extra options with that beaded top and add it to dressy jeans. One of the most fun looks to put together is the androgynous look of combining masculine and feminine. For example, I use the skirt from a navy suit with gold pinstripes and top it with a gold cami and lace jacket. Another time I add a navy cummerbund and take off the jacket, and the gold lace cami becomes the star. Gold accessories and strappy sandals really make the look work.

Dates

Dates can be many things in many places. Knowing specifics is helpful. For athletic events, layering is always sporty. And be mindful there is a difference if you will be sitting in a corporate box vs. infield or general bleacher seating. For a dinner and movie date, donning a sweater or twin-set over your skirt suit or pants will transform your outfit from the office. Jackets change the tone and can be found in a variety of fabrics and styles; velvet, tweeds, military, cropped and the boyfriend blazer. Try them with a camisole, jeans and pumps for a casual yet dressed-up special occasion. Leggings are super paired with pumps, boots, or flats. And of course, the little black dress can be worked in many ways.

A note here about proportions: wear long over short and short over long. Tight over slouchy and baggy over slender. A skirt or dress ought to hit the legs where they curve; above the knee, below the knee, or at the calf.

Cruises and Resorts

Familiarize yourself with the cruise line and be aware that while many are freestyle, some may include an additional restaurant that is more dressy. Bring one dressy dress and a special one for the customary gala evening. For daytime, if you have good legs, wear shorts. Some cruise wear—shorts, cotton tops, sandals, swimsuits—can also be appropriate for resorts. And please gear some of your clothing to any shore excursions. Be mindful of the culture in the countries you visit, not only in terms of your appearance, but for your communication and behavior.

More Parties!

What type of party are you attending? Is there a theme? What will the atmosphere be like? Parties, as we know, run the gamut from casual, sporty, hangout events to elaborate, festive celebrations and everything in between. Soon you will understand that clothing is a tool for personal expression. My positive intent here is to encourage you to adopt an attitude of fun. There is magic in creation.

"People are like stained glass windows. They sparkle and shine when the sun is out, but when the darkness sets in, their true beauty is revealed only if there is a light from within."
—Elisabeth Kübler-Ross, Swiss-born psychiatrist

I like this quote, because it exemplifies for me the importance of being authentic. Being in the world, not of the world. As a licensed cosmetologist and image consultant, I have spent many years in the beauty, fashion, modeling and wellness industries. What I know for sure is that our appearance can be flawless and if we open our mouths and express something mean-spirited, it is for naught.

Special occasions can bring up emotions. Sometimes we can feel more like a role or label as we seek to navigate and interact in society. For that reason, it is imperative that we act with clarity and integrity.

"Let the world know you as you are, not as you think you should be, because sooner or later, if you are posing, you will forget the pose, and then where are you?"
—Fanny Brice, American actress

A Few Final Thoughts

I hope you have received ideas and inspiration to create your signature look. Something I do with my wardrobe may help you glean some inspiration—I have a special occasion go-to section where I put together occasion-specific items, such as a star top and accessories to match or contrast. For example, peau de soie pumps, chandelier earrings, an evening clutch and glitter top with black tuxedo pants, drawstring pants or a pencil skirt. Since your special occasion pieces do not get used as often, you can lose track of them if you do not have a special place set aside. By setting up your special occasion go-to section, you will find it easy to get dressed quickly and easily for each big night.

Use these ideas to create your own special occasion boutique in your closet so you'll be ready to go and know you look fabulous every time you receive that special invitation.

Look great, feel great, have fun and be the dancing star of your life!

MARI BOWLIN, FFS
Spirit of the Style

Empowered style and confidence

(214) 946-3958
mari@spiritofthestyle.com
www.spiritofthestyle.com

*M*ari is a top stylist and has been a leader in the modeling, beauty, fashion, spa and wellness industry for more than 30 years. Known as a visionary with a keen sense of style and panache, Mari's creative talent in fashion and her passion for beauty and wellness has made her one of the area's most sought-after stylists.

As a facilitator with Fashion Feng Shui® International and the International Clarity Institute, she is now bringing her styling expertise to help women *find their spiritual side of style* by providing the spiritual and practical tools to build her clients' inner confidence, self-esteem and beauty. Mari shares her knowledge of both inner and outer beauty via workshops, seminars and retreats internationally.

Her many accomplishments include co-founding a beauty makeover column for the South Bend *Indiana Tribune,* authoring a monthly wellness column, hosting a fashion segment for WSBT and serving as Wellness Director for an Aveda Concept Salon.

The Finishing *Touches* to Your Style

By Ginny Baldridge, MSE, AICI FLC

Your image reflects your goals and dreams, and your goals and dreams reflect your image.

Living in these hectic, busy, modern times, we are inundated with images on television, in movies, on the Internet and in the print media. Throughout the day, we see people in cars, while we shop, when we go to classes and at all the events we attend. Looking fabulous and confidently knowing that you do will literally change your world.

Before You Go Out to Meet The World

Good grooming is the most important aspect of a good appearance and is the area that is neglected when a person doesn't take time to care for herself or has never been taught proper grooming. Good personal hygiene, neat and stylish hair, appropriate makeup, well-manicured nails and clean and well-maintained clothing are all aspects of good grooming.

Heavenly Hair

Having great hair or experiencing a "bad hair day" affects more than your appearance. It impacts your actions, self-assurance and attitude.

Choose a hairstyle that is flattering to your face shape and does not distract from your eyes. Get a really fantastic, *no fuss* haircut. Your hair should be clean and kept free of dandruff. I recommend tea tree shampoos to eliminate this challenge. Develop a good relationship with your hair stylist and schedule regular appointments. When color-enhancing your hair, keep hair roots covered in a timely manner. If you can't get to your roots for a day or two, wear a cap, or use one of the many touch-up products that act as mascara for your hair to cover the grey between salon visits. You can never undo that "awful image" others see when roots are exposed.

Don't forget to clean your brush and comb monthly by soaking them in bleach and warm water. If you use a flat iron, buy one from a beauty supply house or from your hairdresser. An inexpensive flat iron will do irreparable damage to your hair. Be sure to buy hair products formulated for flat iron use to help protect your hair.

Facial Hair Is Never in Style

Invest in a magnifying makeup mirror, especially if your eyes are not as good as they used to be. Once you get over seeing your face magnified to ten times its size, you will appreciate being able to nab that hair you could not see in your bathroom mirror. If you have graying hair, it can be particularly challenging to "see" white or gray hairs. You can get rid of unsightly facial and chin hair easily with a good tweezer.

High, arched eyebrows and thinned brow styles come and go with the trends. This is one area in which you do not want to be a trend follower because keeping your brows shaped in a certain style for over a year or two can prevent the tweezed hair from growing back. Instead, have your eyebrows shaped to open your eyes and face. Choose a good salon that has a specialist in brow shaping and waxing. Once you have had the service, you can often maintain the shape with tweezers or a small scissor for a month or more before having the service repeated. A good eyebrow shaping can make you look younger and in some cases even appear to give you a non-surgical face lift. Do not overlook this potentially minor miracle.

Glowing Skin

You are never too young or too old to start taking care of your skin. Clean, healthy skin is the best thing you can wear on your face. Because we clothe our bodies the majority of the time, we are viewed from our neckline up. So, it makes sense to pay attention to the way our face looks. The most elaborate makeup application cannot compensate for skin that is not cared for. Treat your skin accordingly to its type—dry, normal, oily or combination.

The first step is cleansing morning and night with a water-soluble cleanser that lifts dirt and then rinses away with warm water. Toning follows cleansing to re-establish the skin's pH balance and close pores. Choose cleanser, toner and moisturizer that match your skin type. Exfoliating removes dead cells from the skin's surface and should be done periodically with an abrasive scrub or daily with an alpha-hydroxy acid product. Moisturizing softens and re-hydrates the skin, keeping it supple and preventing wrinkles. For dry skin or rosacea, work with a specialist to determine the best treatment for your skin.

Sunscreen should be applied every day to exposed skin, and not just if you are going to be in the sun. UVB rays cannot penetrate glass windows, but UVA rays can, leaving your skin prone to these damaging effects if unprotected. For days when you are going to be indoors, apply sunscreen on the areas not covered by clothing, such as the face and hands. Sunscreens can be applied under makeup, or choose one of the many cosmetic products available that contain sunscreens for daily use. Sun protection is the principal means of preventing premature aging and skin cancer. It's never too late to protect yourself from the sun and minimize your future risk of skin cancer. Lip balms prevent lips from drying out, but do little to replenish lost moisture.

Bright Teeth

Americans are among the most teeth-conscious people on earth, so we feel surprised or repulsed when someone has unattractive, unhealthy or crooked teeth. Brush at least twice a day. Flossing daily will prevent gum disease and eliminates 90 percent of mouth odor as decayed food is removed more effectively. Using a whitener can take years off your age. Some procedures cost hundreds of dollars, but there are effective, inexpensive whitening products available over the counter that—if used regularly—leave your teeth whiter.

Keep breath fresh. If you chew gum, it should not be obvious to others. I cannot emphasize how distracting it is to view someone who is smacking on their gum. I suggest you chew gum if it is needed to freshen your breath and then dispose of it right away if you are going to be chatting with others.

Oh, the Tattoos

Tattoos have a long history. The period from 1960 to the 1990s became known as the age of "prison tats." During the 1980s many professional athletes starting sporting tattoos. Today, tattoos have become a growing fad. Do understand that a tattoo may effectively prohibit you from pursuing a professional career, regardless of your other qualifications. Keeping in mind that as women, we always want to keep attention focused on our faces, so I suggest steering away from being tattooed. If you have one, recognize that no matter how much you like it and like to show it off, it may not always get you the reaction you like and may not be making the impression you want. There is nothing wrong with covering it up in certain situations.

Eyeglasses

Squinting looks good on no one. Yet the wrong eyeglass frame can make you look matronly or geeky. Give special consideration to selecting your spectacles. Eyeglass frames are an awesome accessory and their styles change almost as often as clothing styles. Have an image consultant or eyewear consultant go with you to find the perfect shape that best fits your face shape and personality. It is important to keep your eyeglasses clean and free of dirt and smudges, a noticeable and tell-tale sign of indifference to your appearance.

For tips on choosing the best eyeglass frames, see Michele Bayle's chapter, *What Do Your Glasses Say About You?* on page 189.

Nail Care

Great nails are clean with no chipped polish, filed evenly, free of hangnails and a consistent shape. To help keep them that way, wear protective gloves when you work around your home.

There is nothing more unsightly than a well-dressed woman with painted nails that are way overdue for a redo. You have a decision to make: nail polish or no nail polish? If you are too busy or do not want to take the time to keep up with the base coat, color coat and top coat, then go bare. Nude nails are fine if they are well cared for. If you are rushed to prepare for an event, you can add some clear polish or use "press-on" nails. They will last through the event and are easy to remove.

Hold On to Your Hands

Most of us do not often think about our hands. Yet others see them all day long and it is important to take good care of them. For beautiful hands, use hand lotion morning and night. Place a lotion pump at the kitchen sink and remember to use it after cleaning and cooking. And remember the tip about wearing protective gloves when cleaning or using water for an extended time.

Step Back Five Feet

Bad breath, chronic halitosis or body odor can be very unpleasant and ruin your whole day. Smokers particularly need to keep Listerine® tabs or breath mints on hand. A daily bath or shower must be a part of your personal routine and provides remarkable emotional benefits as well. To control more difficult body odor problems, keep underarm hair shaved to eliminate a breeding ground for bacteria. Use a good deodorant or antiperspirant—it may take trying several brands to find the one that works for you. Using your favorite fragrance may give you a real lift. Be careful not to use too much as some people have allergies and are affected by strong fragrances.

The Most Obvious Accessory

Your purse or bag is the most seen accessory and can be the most "fun" accessory. Choose your handbag in proportion to your body size—smaller purses for small women and a larger bag for larger women. You also want to choose a length of shoulder strap that allows your bag to swing above the hip. Keep your handbags neat and in good shape, including the interior of the bag. If you have papers, receipts, tissues, keys, phone, and coupons hanging out of your purse, you will be viewed as messy and disorganized. Take a few minutes weekly to manage the contents of your purse. Keep receipts in a small closed envelope. For any other paper items that need to remain in your purse, keep them folded and in a small snack size zipper-lock bag. Keep makeup items in a small, zippered makeup bag.

You will be surprised how keeping your things organized inside your purse can make your day go easier. If you keep items bundled it makes changing purses a lot easier.

For going to work, you may choose to carry a classic neutral color handbag, such as black, brown or navy. I love to have bags that are colorful and that match my ensemble. In the spring and summer, lighter fabrics in pinks, yellows, or pastel blues are a good idea. In the colder months, leather, suede or sateen or metallic leathers are best. Have fun choosing a purse that matches your personality and wardrobe style.

A Favorite Motto—Be Prepared

Even in today's casual atmosphere, you may want to keep panty hose, polished shoes, and a clean and pressed dress handy. You never know when there will be a last-minute cocktail party you are invited to attend, an honor ceremony for your child or a funeral that requires your presence. You will want to respect the situation and dress appropriately. I enjoy knowing that I have a classic necklace or bracelet and earrings (such as faux pearls) on hand to go with a classic black dress.

Owning an evening wrap is always a good idea as it can be used instead of a coat or jacket, will complement your outfit and can keep you warm in a cool environment. In addition to black, try wearing a pink or red wrap with your dress to add a little finesse to your outfit.

There are a variety of steamers on the market today. I suggest investing in one because it is so difficult to find time to actually iron. A quick steam will remove obvious wrinkles from any fabric. In a pinch, try hanging your garments in the bathroom as you shower. Another quick fix for smudged or dirty shoes is to use a disposable shoeshine towelette. They come in a one-inch square packet and can be used for a clear wax shine.

The Last-Minute Check

Before you go out, check in a full-length mirror in a lighted room for fallen hems, missing buttons, wrinkles, stains or panty lines. Be sure your garments are not too tight or too huge. If you notice panty lines, either change into a pant that fits more loosely or grab a jacket that covers your hips. Women's lingerie departments now carry various forms of "no line" panties, These can prevent your underwear from slipping up your hips and give a nice smooth look. If you have lost weight and your clothes are saggy, try adding a belt to cinch everything at your waist. Baggy clothing can make you seem to be lacking in self-confidence. Pay attention to your silhouette in your winter coat. Stuffing the pockets with gloves, tissue or hats will add bulk to your form. Keep a lint roller on hand for a quick once-over on any dark-colored slacks, skirt or coat. These items tend to show lint, and it can easily be removed in less than five seconds.

For Emergencies

I am not suggesting you carry "every item imaginable" in your purse, but following is a list of items that could save you from deep embarrassment. Most of these can be kept together in a small bag inside your purse or kept handy in your car.

Emergency Kit Contents

- Small scissor, nail trimmer, emery board
- Small foldaway umbrella
- Aspirin or other pain reliever
- Energy bar or granola bar
- Scarf—to cover a ruined blouse
- Makeup kit, mirror, brush and hair spray
- Floss and breath mints
- Tissues
- Tiny packet of Shout® or similar stain-removing wipes
- Tiny lint brush
- Hand sanitizer
- Sanitary napkins or tampons
- Safety pins, extra button
- Hand lotion

Before you go out, apply lipstick to achieve an uplifted look and put confidence in your gorgeous smile.

Taking a few extra minutes daily to give more attention to your grooming will increase your self-assurance. You will walk, talk and think differently. It will have others noticing the positive change in your appearance and responding accordingly. Use your beautiful smile and make eye contact as often as possible; it may be the only positive thing that happens in another person's day.

GINNY BALDRIDGE, MSE, AICI FLC
Your Style

*Helping people look and feel great,
do better in life, and achieve their
personal and professional goals*

(314) 952-8488
ginny@yourstyleginny.com
www.yourstyleginny.com

*G*inny makes learning about image and its do's and don'ts a fun and powerful event. Ginny's southern grace and charm are sure to warm your heart and leave you feeling happy to have spent time with her.

Working with businesses, she presents workshops and seminars on professional and casual dress. Your Style image services are designed to benefit the business professional, the volunteer, or the busy stay-at-home mom. Ginny also specializes in helping cancer patients and survivors with the image challenges unique to their situation. "A positive attitude can affect the outcome to your treatment."

Ginny is certified by the Association of Image Consultants International. She holds a Masters of Education, is an Elegance In Style graduate, served as Board Member of Family Enrichment International for eight years, is a member of National Speakers Association and an Executive Member of Fashion Group International. She co-authored *Executive Image Power,* published by PowerDynamics Publishing in 2009, has appeared on the *Great Day in St. Louis* television show and delivers popular workshops for the Working Women's Survival Show.

More INSPIRED *Style*

*N*ow that you have learned many things about how to discover your personal style, the next step is to take action. Get started applying what you have learned in the pages of this book.

We want you to know that we are here to help and inspire you to become your best and most stylish self.

Following is a list of where we are geographically located. Regardless of where our companies are located, many of us provide a variety of services over the phone or through webinars, and we welcome the opportunity to travel to your location to provide you one-on-one style consulting.

You can find out more about each of us by reading our bios at the end of our chapters, or by visiting our websites, listed below.

If you are looking for one-on-one coaching or group training, many of the co-authors in this book are available to support you. Feel free to call us and let us know you have read our book and let us know how to best serve you.

United States

Arizona

Lisa Ann Martin   www.lisashops.com
                                          www.stealthstyling.com

California

Pat Gray, PhD, AICI FLC   www.patgrayincolor.com
Barbara Layne, PhD   www.makeupandfashion.info

Colorado

Milena Joy   www.milenaconsulting.com

Florida

Oreet Mizrahi, AICI FLC   www.mizrahiimage.com

Kansas

Cynthia Lee Miller, AICI FLC   www.cynthialeemiller.com

Kentucky

Chris Fulkerson   www.vipstudioonline.com

Massachusetts

Debbie Wright   www.projectcloset.com

Michigan

Julie Maeder, AICI FLC   www.newleafimageconsulting.com
Alison Vaughn   www.jacketsforjobs.org

Minnesota
Carrie Leum

www.corsetstyling.com

Missouri
Ginny Baldridge, MSE, AICI FLC

www.yourstyleginny.com

Cheryl Obermiller

www.classicimageconsulting.com

Oregon
Sandy Moore, AICI CIP

www.imagetalks.com

Texas
Mari Bowlin, FFS

www.spiritofthestyle.com

Sally Templeton

www.sallytdesigns.com

Washington
Michele Bayle, LDO

www.wink-eyewear.com

Canada

British Columbia
Deborah Reynolds

www.aboutfaceimage.com

Alberta
Shirley Borrelli

www.shirleyborrelli.com

Ontario
Teresa McCarthy, AICI FLC

www.imagesolutionsgroup.ca

Dominique Vaughan-Russell, AICI FLC

www.vaughanrussell.com

PowerDynamics Publishing develops books for experts who want to share their knowledge with more and more people.

We provide experts with a proven system, guidance and support to produce quality multi-author how to books to uplift and enhance the personal and professional lives of the people they serve.

We know getting a book written and published is a huge project. We provide the resources, know-how and an experienced team to put a quality, informative book in the hands of our co-authors quickly and affordably. We provide books, in which our co-authors are proud to be included, that serve to enhance their business missions.

You can find out more about our upcoming book projects at
www.powerdynamicspub.com

Also from
PowerDynamics Publishing

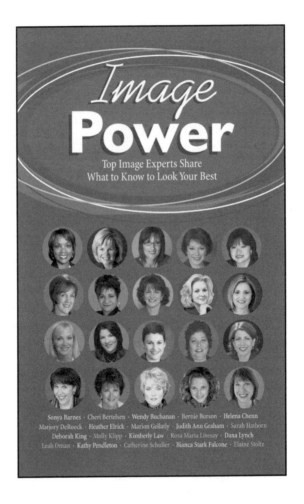

For more information on this book visit:
www.imagepowerbook.com

Also from
PowerDynamics Publishing

Top Image Experts Share What to Know to Advance Your Career

EXECUTIVE

IMAGE

POWER

Colleen Abrie · Yasmin Anderson-Smith · Ginny Baldridge · Joanne Blake · Jennifer Bressie
Karen Brunger · Amy Elizabeth Casson · Betty Chu · Julie Kaufman · Kathryn Lowell
Suzanne Mauro · Maureen Merrill · Brenda Moore-Frazier · Peggy M. Parks · Beverly Samuel
Lauren Solomon · Anne Sowden · Beth Thorp · Divya Vashi · Cynthia Bruno Wynkoop

For more information on this book visit:
www.executiveimagebook.com

Also from
PowerDynamics Publishing

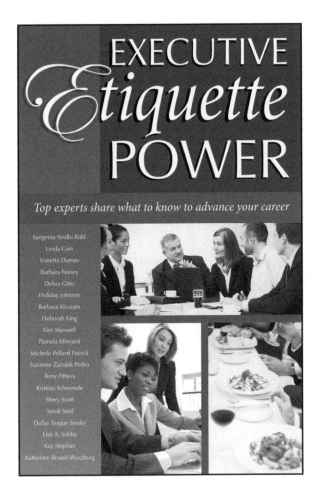

For more information on this book visit:
www.execetiquette.com

Also from
PowerDynamics Publishing

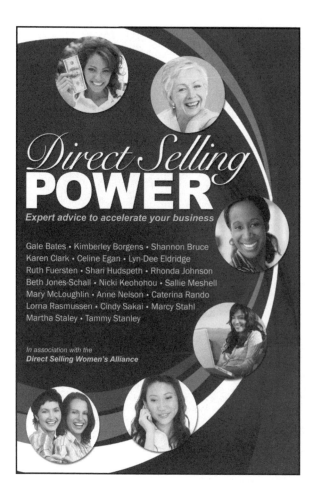

For more information on this book visit:
www.directsellingpower.com

TOP IMAGE EXPERTS
reveal strategies to always
look and be your best

INSPIRED
Style

Ginny Baldridge • Michele Bayle • Shirley Borrelli • Mari Bowlin
Chris Fulkerson • Pat Gray • Milena Joy • Barbara Layne • Carrie Leum
Julie Maeder • Lisa Ann Martin • Teresa McCarthy • Cynthia Lee Miller
Oreet Mizrahi • Sandy Moore • Cheryl Obermiller • Deborah Reynolds
Sally Templeton • Dominique Vaughan-Russell • Alison Vaughn • Debbie Wright

For more copies of *Inspired Style*,
contact any of the co-authors or visit:
www.inspiredstylebook.com